YOU Can Heal Within

YOU Can Heal Within

Joanne Plater

First published 2025 by The Kind Press
Copyright © Joanne Plater 2025

All rights reserved. No part of this book may be reproduced by any mechanical, photographic or electronic process, including AI-generated reproductions, or in the form of a phonographic recording, nor may it be stored in a retrieval system, transmitted, or otherwise copied for public or private use other than for 'fair use' as brief quotations embodied in articles and reviews without prior written permission from the publisher.

 A catalogue record for this book is available from the National Library of Australia

ISBN: 9781763800939 (paperback)
ISBN: 9781763800946 (eBook)

Disclaimer

This book is provided for informational and inspirational purposes only and is not intended as a substitute for psychological, financial, medical or other professional advice. The author's intention is to offer information of a general nature to support your journey towards emotional, physical and spiritual wellbeing. However, individual circumstances vary, and readers should seek guidance from appropriately qualified professionals where necessary. If you are experiencing severe emotional distress, depression or any mental health concerns, please consult a registered mental health professional. This book is not a substitute for therapy, counselling or psychiatric care. By choosing to apply the information in this book, you acknowledge that you do so at your own discretion and risk. Neither the author nor the publisher accepts any liability for loss, damage or disruption resulting from the use of, or reliance upon, any information contained in this book. This includes, but is not limited to, direct, indirect, incidental, special or consequential damages.

Important Safety Notice

The meditation techniques and practices described in this book are intended for use in a calm, safe and distraction-free environment. **Do not practise meditation while driving, operating heavy machinery or performing any task that requires your full attention.** Always ensure you are in an appropriate setting before engaging in any meditative or contemplative practice.

To my beautiful husband and best friend Elliot, thank you for always encouraging, loving and supporting me in all of my ideas and accepting me and my heavenly spiritual team.

To my beautiful children, who make my heart fill with joy. You make me want to be my best version of myself and for me to be brave and show them that you can achieve anything you set your mind to.

To my clients and students, who I love helping, guiding and healing. I'm so blessed to be able to help and hold space for other spiritually like-minded people.

To myself for being brave enough to put pen to paper and put myself out in the big wide world and not hide away in the beautiful town of Bellingen NSW Australia.

Thank you to my spiritual team for picking me to help others, my best friends in the astrals.

Contents

Introduction   1
How to Use This Book   3
Reading the Book   6
Reading for Others   8

PART ONE: Clearing Negative Emotions

1 Accepting You   13
2 Chakra Repair   15
3 DNA Release   18
4 Forgiveness   21
5 Guilty   23
6 Habit Healing   25
7 Impatience   27
8 Past Lovers and Friends   28
9 Pink Bubble Healing   30
10 Poverty Thoughts   32
11 Procrastination   34
12 Relationship Purge   35
13 Positive Self Talk   37
14 Shadow Self-Clearing   39

PART TWO: Motivational Messages

15 Abundance	43
16 Bucket List	44
17 Do It, Do it!	45
18 Grace, Rise above it	46
19 Gratitude	47
20 Gut Instinct, Trust	48
21 Look Forward	49
22 Lovers	50
23 Manifesting	52
24 Wealth	54
25 Surrender	55

PART THREE: Body

26 Detox	59
27 Detox Technology	61
28 Protection	62
29 Rest and Recover	63
30 Water	64

PART FOUR: Magic and Mystery

31 Celebrations	67
32 Divine Timing	68
33 Goals and Dreams	69
34 Power	70
35 Signs	71

PART FIVE: Your Team

36 Dragons	75
37 The Elementals	77
38 Meeting your Spirit Guide	79
39 Unicorns	81

40 Heavenly Family Member — 83
41 Universal Healing — 84

PART SIX: Chakra Healing

42 Base Chakra — 87
43 Sacral Chakra — 90
44 Solar Plexus Chakra — 93
45 Heart Chakra — 96
46 Throat Chakra — 99
47 Third Eye Chakra — 102
48 Crown Chakra — 105
49 Higher Self Chakra — 108
50 Earth Star Chakra — 111

PART SEVEN: Activating Your Intuition and Clairs

51 Clairvoyant — 115
52 Clairsentience — 117
53 Clairaudience — 119
54 Claircognition — 121
55 Intuition and Gut Instinct — 123

PART EIGHT: Inner Children

56 Inner Child 0–7 — 127
57 Inner Child 7–14 — 129
58 Inner Child 14–21 — 132

PART NINE: Healing

59 House Clearing — 137
60 Living with Gratitude — 139
61 Past Life Clearing — 141
62 Vagus Nerve — 143
63 Vibrating High — 145

64 Medicine Healing	146
65 Ancestry Healing	147
66 Limbic Healing	149
67 Timeline Healing	150

PART TEN: Archangels

68 Archangel Ariel	153
69 Archangel Mary	155
70 Jesus – Christ Light	157
71 Archangel Gabriel	159
72 Archangel Metatron	161
73 Archangel Michael	163
74 Archangel Nathaniel	165
75 Archangel Raphael	167
76 Archangel Raziel	169
77 Miriam Ascended Master	171

PART ELEVEN: The Alchemist Within

78 Sorcerer	175
79 Chemistry Within	176
80 Enchanted	178
81 Soul's Journey	179
82 Your Holy Grail	180
83 Trinity Healing	181
84 The Magi	182
85 Master Lives	183
86 Goddess of Opportunity Lady Portia	185
87 Calling in your Higher Guidance	188
88 Untangled Energy	190
89 Merlin Dragon	192
90 Earth Star Abundance	194
91 Unicorn Healing	196

92 Sun Strength	198
93 Full Moon Energy	199
94 New Moon Healing	200
95 Sovereignty Within	201
96 Becoming Self Sufficient and Respecting Mother Earth	202
About the Author	205

Introduction

This book was inspired by information gathered during my one-on-one healing sessions. It represents what I have helped to heal in others and the topics I discuss most with my clients. This book contains the soul lessons we have come to Earth to learn.

This book will help you learn about your chakras, childhood emotions, intuition, and how to activate your Clair senses. You will get to know your spiritual team, learn who you can work with, and open your communication with the Archangels and angels who are here to help you. It is a powerful way to connect with and receive signs and symbols from your spiritual family and passed-over loved ones, guiding you towards your best life.

It will support you in healing limiting habits that may be preventing your transformation into your higher self. You can use this book to release bad habits and clear negative thought patterns, allowing you to connect with your spirit and higher self to facilitate healing within yourself and others.

Now more than ever, the veil between the spiritual realm and Earth is at its thinnest. If you have this book in your hands, it is time to explore and connect with the spiritual realms. Reading a passage daily is the simplest way to begin connecting with the spiritual realm and healing from within. Use this book to clear away negative thoughts and emotions to raise your vibration. When you raise your vibration, you in turn collectively raise the vibration of Earth.

There are no coincidences in life, only signs and symbols from the universe to help you learn your life lessons and live your best life.

Joanne Plater

How to Use This Book

This book is a source of guidance, offering insights from the universe, these pages hold wisdom to support you on your soul's journey, helping you connect with your intuition, receive divine messages, and raise your vibration.

You can use this book in many ways:

- Open to a random page and trust that the message you land on is exactly what you need in this moment.
- Read a passage daily to set an intention for your day.
- To discover what your angelic guides want you to work on. (I often keep coming back to the same message until I truly start to work on what they advise.)
- Ask a question and allow your guides to lead you to the answer within these pages.
- Use it for deeper reflection during meditation or journaling.
- Turn to it during the full moon to release what no longer serves you, or during the new moon to set new intentions.

There is no right or wrong way to use this book. Trust your intuition and let the words guide you. Some messages may resonate instantly, while others may unfold over time. Allow the wisdom within these pages to support you as you navigate your personal and spiritual growth.

If this book has found its way into your hands, know that it is not by chance. You are being called to heal, to grow, and to listen to the guidance that has always been within you. If any words or phrases seem to jump out at you, pay close attention. This is a sign from the angels and your guides showing you what you need to look at in your life.

If you are a psychic, clairvoyant, or spiritual practitioner, you can use this book to help with clients. You can hold the book and ask Archangel Michael to clear the energy of the previous readings. You can then ask universe healers to help guide you to the right pages to best help your client (saying their name).

You can place this book on top of some amethyst or selenite to help rejuvenate its energy. I always keep a copy in my healing room or in my handbag. I personally love using spiritual books and oracle decks for guidance and have often turned to them throughout my life for support.

If you are a full moon or new moon person, these are great times to do a reading for yourself. At the full moon, ask what you need to purge or let go of. If it is a new moon, ask, What do I need to work on? Sometimes, I will write my question on paper, place the question inside the book, and then place both on top of some beautiful crystals, asking the universe to help me with the answers.

You can do a reading for a particular area of your life, e.g., relationships, career, friends. I personally love doing a 12-month reading for the year ahead by choosing a passage for each month. I will then write them on my vision board so I can see what each month will represent from the book. You may choose to simply write them in your journal or Spiritual Diary to remind you each month which path your inner healing needs to follow. When doing a 12-month forecast, I do separate readings for my personal life and my business/career. Energetically, these are very different worlds, and it is important to clearly divide the two in order to receive clarity from the readings.

I urge you to also let your intuitive guidance come through when interpreting your reading. Go with the first feelings or emotions you have when you read the passage. Start to trust your intuition.

Reading the Book

Before you use the book, you may want to bless the book. Holding the book in your hands, ask your spirit guides and angels to bless these pages with the highest guidance and wisdom, as well as to help you and guide you on your soul's journey in this lifetime.

Flip through the pages in whatever manner feels right for you – this may be a basic flip-through, an intentional selection, or simply allowing the book to fall open to a certain page. Also, turn through the pages for however long feels right for you. (Remember, if a page stands out, always go with it.) Choosing the page that is calling you can be done in a number of ways. You may simply read the page the book opens to. If any section slightly stands out or catches your attention, you could start there. You may fan through the book, hovering your hand over the pages to feel which one pulls you in. That is the beauty of this book – there is no correct way to choose, it is only what feels right for you.

Once you have your page or pages, read the passage and reflect on its meaning. Sometimes, the message will resonate instantly, and you will know exactly why that page was calling you. However, be sure to read thoroughly, as even though it may not seem obvious right now, it may unfold later in the day or week. That's the excitement in the magic and mystery of the messages. Trust what your guides are showing you – it will lead to awakening and enlightenment on your soul's journey here on Earth.

Reading for Others

If you are doing a reading for someone else, I advise you to ask Archangel Michael to clear the book of any overlaid energy from you and clear the pages to give the best reading for (say their name). Once you have finished the reading for your client or friend, ask Archangel Michael once again to clear the book. If you have any Rose Quartz Crystals, Amethyst or Selenite, place them around your book. Each month, place your book in the light of the full moon if possible. If that is unachievable, place the book on a large piece of Amethyst to clear old energies and keep its vibration high.

YOU'LL ALSO FIND GUIDED MEDITATIONS THROUGHOUT THE BOOK.

QR codes are included so you can easily access audio content, following your reading with a meditation can help you understand and integrate the message. Joanne Plater has a full list of guided meditations for subscription online that you may find useful in your integration.

Go the website www.joanneplater.com.au

PART ONE

Clearing Negative Emotions

1 Accepting You

You have turned to this page to remind yourself to accept yourself as a divine creation of God or the universe.

You are prefect just as you are, you do not need to compare yourself to anyone. Everyone on Earth is here for their own soul lessons and soul's journey. One of your biggest lessons here on Earth is to accept yourself just as you are.

If you are wanting to start going on dates or find a partner, launch or publish a book, maybe start a business, however you feel you need to lose weight, get some part of your body fixed or whatever it is that you think is holding you back, please stop these thought patterns and start anyway. Fix whatever it is about you along the way if you feel you need to. But START. You can start to improve yourself if you wish, but do not stop or hold yourself back by the lack of acceptance within yourself. If you learn to love yourself just as you are so will others. Most humans on the planet don't like something about themselves, even the people you think are perfect. All humans, through their own eyes have something they don't like about their body. Whatever your age, it is a privilege to be that age – enjoy it. Someone who has a terminal illness isn't counting wrinkles or despising crooked teeth, they would be grateful for your body, simply because it is healthy.

Your spirit guides, your higher self, and the Archangels, want you to start to like and eventually love yourself for who you are, right now. You can start to accept yourself by being grateful for all your body parts.

Thank yourself for being able to walk around today, what great feet and legs I have.

Thank your mouth, teeth, and tongue for chewing my food and helping to nourish my body, for giving me voice, and to kiss my kids goodnight.

Look at these hands that can hold other people's hands, help other people, and help myself with my career and to survive here on Earth.

The examples above, we can all take for granted. Start being grateful for the basics your body provides you with and then start to be grateful for more of your individual body parts. Remember the terminally ill person, live your best life and that means to start to love and accept yourself just as you are.

Love and accept yourself like a good friend would. Your spirit guides, higher self and Archangels do. Live the life you have imaged in your mind and do not hold yourself back by the vessel (body) you have been given.

2 Chakra Repair

If you have turned to this page, it is a sign to learn how to do a quick chakra repair on yourself.

This exercise is best to be one in a private place. E.g., your car, a closed office or alone in your home. If you feel drained from a meeting, phone call, text message, email or a group situation or have been shopping in a large, busy shopping centre, you will most likely feel the need to recalibrate. This chakra balance or chakra repair is a great way to clear negative energy from other humans or from overlaid energy from places you have visited.

1. Ask God or the divine creator for a column of white light through your whole body, expanding the white light about 1 metre around you.
2. Ask your spirit guide to step into the column with you. Even if you do not feel their presence, please ask anyway.
3. Ask Archangel Michael to step in the white light column you are in and clear away any overlaid energy from other people, any lost souls, or any negative entities. Takes some deep breaths and allow Archangel Michael to clear them away.
4. Ask God or the divine creator for the column of light you are standing in to change to a rainbow column of light. The rainbow healing energy from God or the divine creator is healing every cell of your body. Take some deep breaths and breath the rainbow energy all through your body.
5. Focus now on your base chakra and imagine or feel the rainbow energy is healing and adding extra energy needed to your base chakra.

6. Focus now on your sacral chakra and imagine or feel the rainbow energy is healing and adding extra energy needed to your sacral chakra.
7. Focus now on your solar plexus chakra and imagine or feel the rainbow energy is healing and adding extra energy needed to your solar plexus chakra.
8. Focus now on your heart chakra and imagine or feel the rainbow energy is healing and adding extra energy needed to your heart chakra.
9. Focus now on your throat chakra and imagine or feel the rainbow energy is healing and adding extra energy needed to your throat chakra.
10. Focus now on your third eye chakra and imagine or feel the rainbow energy is healing and adding extra energy needed to your third eye chakra.
11. Focus now on your crown chakra and imagine or feel the rainbow energy is healing and adding extra energy needed to your crown chakra.
12. Now Ask Archangel Raphael to step into your column and heal any chakras that need repairing and any chakras that need extra healing from Archangel Raphael.
13. Ask Archangel Michael for his blue healing cloak of protection, to keep your energy cleared and protected from others.
14. Thank yourself, God or the divine creator, Archangel Michael, and Archangel Raphael for their healing today.

This exercise is great to do, especially when you feel drained. You can also do it morning and night to keep your vibration and energy high. Repeat this exercise anytime your body feels drained or has been compromised by others.

SCAN THE QR CODE FOR A
GUIDED CHAKRA BALANCE MEDITATION

After the meditation, if you feel guided, journal your thoughts, feelings and emotions from the meditation.

3 DNA Release

If you have turned to this page, it is time to acknowledge and release inherited patterns of abuse, poverty consciousness, lack of positive thinking, alcoholism, obesity (emotional overeating), negativity (the glass or situation is always half empty).

Many families hold shame, embarrassment, guilt or fear within our emotional and energetic nervous system. It is as though the family DNA is holding the fight or flight response. Some family lineages hold karmic debts around money or the curse of past lovers. They are easily definable by a family line of unhappy marriages, generations of unlucky business ventures or a great monetary lack.

Below is the visualisation to guide you through a DNA release. You may choose to read it in its entirety, then sit with the meditation, or you can read a line or two at a time, digesting and incorporating each element as you go.

DNA RELEASE STEPS

Take a moment to settle your body and find a comfortable position.

Take three deep breaths, in through the nose and out through the mouth.

Ask God or the Divine Creator for a column of white light to be sent all the way through your body. Continue to breathe and tune into the vibration of the white light.

Ask Archangel Michael to clear the following:

- any terminal illness from your family's DNA and any genetic forms of cancer
- any deformities or abnormalities that have occurred within your family tree
- any physical issues that have been passed down through your family
- any karma associated with poverty consciousness, asking that you no longer need to be poor or wear the family's karma. Ask for this to be cleared away for you and your living family
- any karma associated with money and karmic debt to money. This includes any debts of money that your ancestors may have accrued
- any karma associated with mental illness or suicidal tendencies, or shame associated with anyone who has suicided in your family history. Ask that this energy be removed from your family
- any karma associated with addictions to alcohol, drugs or any other obsessive behaviours. We ask for this DNA to be removed from your body
- any karma, embarrassment or shame to be removed from your family associated with sexual tendencies or relationship ambiguity. For example, children out of wedlock (ancestral shame), highly sexual women or the non-acceptance of homosexuality
- remove any sexual or physical abuse in your family DNA
- remove any curses or ill wishes, whether between family members or from other people.

Now take the time to ask for anything else that you would like to remove for yourself and your family that has not already been mentioned. Letting it all wash away, take some deep breaths and feel all of this leave your body now.

The white light from God or the Divine Creator energy is now resetting your DNA for love, abundance, health, wealth, joy, prosperity consciousness, friendships, successful careers and anything else you want to add into your DNA.

Ask Archangel Michael to reset all these energies and thank him for all his blessings today.

SCAN THE QR CODE FOR A DNA RELEASE MEDITATION

4 Forgiveness

*By turning to this page, it is time for forgiveness.
Let go of the anger and resentment you
have for a family member, friend, lover
or anyone you hold anger toward.*

Often, when you are angry at someone, those feelings of anger are making you sick and low in vibration and energy. You are the soul that is walking around hurt and unhappy. You are not vibrating at your highest energy and with joy and happiness in your soul. Don't give that person or situation, permission over you to destroy your peace and happiness. When you are holding onto anger towards a person or situation, your thoughts are thinking about the past. The guides are wanting you to be present in the moment you are in. They want you to have happy thoughts about yourself and your future. We cannot change our past, but we can forgive and let go of the emotions associated with it.

Ways to let go and forgive:

- A purge letter is a great way to write down how you feel, and then physically release it. Once written, burn the letters and let all the feelings go. As the words burn away, so does your connection to them.
- Starting to meditate is a good way to help forgive and let go.
- Swearing the worst swear words while walking at the beach (providing no one can hear), or swearing in your car when no ones with you.

- Throwing rocks into a lake, dam, river or at the beach. As you throw the rocks, you are letting go of toxic energy and forgiving the person or situation.

Remember, sometimes our soul lessons have nothing to do with the person who has done you wrong but with how you can let go. Learning to forgive and have peace within your soul allows you to disassociate from what has happened in our lives. Do not give them your power and energy or your time in your brain. Forgive them for own your inner peace and wellbeing, so you have a healthy mind and body.

SCAN THE QR CODE FOR THE PAST RELATIONSHIPS MEDITATION

5 Guilty

Are you always feeling guilty about your past or your current situation? You have turned to this page as the universe is asking you to let go of your guilt. You cannot change the past. If you are feeling guilty about your current situation, ask yourself what steps you can take to help ease the guilt you are feeling.

Take some time to let go of the guilt you are feeling. You are doing the best you could of at the time. Whatever has happened in the past or in the present, try to let go of all the guilt you are feeling. Parents often have guilt as to whether they are parenting well. If you have done your best, then that's all you can do. If you felt you have made a bad decision in the past, it's time to forgive yourself for those decisions. When you made those or that decision, you made the best educated decision you could at the time.

The angels are asking you to let go and start to enjoy the rest of your life. Guilt is like carrying around a large suitcase labelled guilty, dragging it around for the rest of your life. Holding that energy is exhausting. Let go, be free. Embrace the decision you have made and forgive yourself. Lay on the grass. Take deep breathes and allow Mother Earth to absorb your guilt. Soak in a river or ocean and let the water clear out your guilt. These are some great physical tools to help let yourself off the hook or clear away/lessen the guilty feeling from your body.

SCAN THE QR CODE FOR THE PURGING MEDITATION

6 Habit Healing

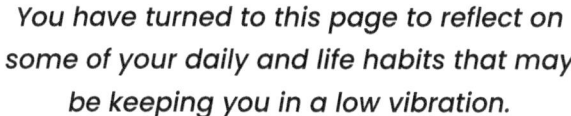

You have turned to this page to reflect on some of your daily and life habits that may be keeping you in a low vibration.

This can include many things, poor eating, poor sleep habits, numbing yourself with drugs, alcohol, too much social media, too much online streaming or possibly even too much reality tv or porn. Gossiping negatively about friends, family or workmates. Wishing ill wishes on people you do not like or have done wrong by you. Being judgemental of others who are not in a great position. Gambling, internet shopping, overspending to make yourself feel better. Even a job you do not like and do 5 days a week. Being in a relationship where you talk negatively about or even to each other, where the relationship is not working together as a team on the same life path. All these habits above are lowering your vibration and you are not living your best soul life.

Start to write a list, just for your eyes only, of all the habits you need to heal in your life. Next to the habit write down a solution or a positive replacement for the habit. Some ways to help change the negative habit is not place yourself in the environment. E.g. if you have a habit of drinking alcohol every day, start to cut back or do not buy any to have in your home. If you want to catch up with friends and family, change the time you catch up and catch up for a healthy breakfast or have a walking/talking catchup with your friend. If you are spending too much time on social media, set a timer in your phone to enjoy 20 mins a day and once the timer goes off, that's it for the day. Instead listen to positive pod casts or read or listen to audio books, something that's adding value to your life.

If you have poor sleep habits set a timer and at that timer you stop anything to do with your phone/TV/social media and start to whine down to get ready for bed.

We are here for such a short time, why waste it with habits that are not enhancing your life or adding value to your soul! It takes time and effort to change negative habits, but you bought this oracle book to heal yourself and become a better version of you. Start small and everyday make changes for a more positive lifestyle.

SCAN THE QR CODE FOR THE LIFTING YOUR VIBRATIONAL ENERGY MEDITATION

7 Impatience

Are you feeling impatient, short-tempered, or overly reactive in your interactions? This is not who you truly are, now is the time to return to your kind, caring, and authentic self.

This page is a reminder to lighten up. Life is short and part of your journey is to connect and communicate with other souls. Remember that it takes more energy to be cranky, grouchy, and impatient, than to feel love, happiness and joy. Stop being a cactus. Maybe you need to take some time in nature to exhale and centre your heart back to being loved focused. If you are cranky with someone, which we all experience occasionally, sleep on it over night before you have a difficult conversation. Sometimes the next day, it does not seem as bad as your first thought. Your anger and impatience are compromising the beautiful soul that you are. No one likes hanging around a painful prickly soul.

SCAN THE QR CODE FOR THE PURGING MEDITATION

8 Past Lovers and Friends

Are you reminiscing about past lovers or old friends? Looking back on relationships that are no longer meant for you will not serve you. It is time to let go, stop dwelling on the past, and release thoughts that keep drawing you back to them. They are in your past.

It could be that you still have overlaid energy or an energy cord connecting you to them. Or it could be that you have had a spiritual contract together in this lifetime. One that was planned in the heavens before you integrated into this lifetime and either one of you did not honour or hold up to the contract. Therefore, it is hard to get over or stop thinking of them.

Ask Archangel Michael for his special clearing with the following words:

> 'Archangel Michael, please disconnect me from (say their name) and de cord the energy between us. I also ask for protection to stop them overlaying me with their energy.
>
> Archangel Michael, if we had a contract together to be lovers or friends in this lifetime, can you please help us reconnect or can you please have this contract given back to us, to sort out for another life or soul journey together.' Thank Archangel Michael for his help.

Purging the relationship, will also help you move on. Another way to purge is a Do Not Send Letter to the person or experience you had. Expressing in the letter your sadness, anger, shame, resentment, humiliation, betrayal, hurt, abandonment. Whatever negative emotions you are feeling. Once you have written the letter, then you burn the letter and as it is burning you let all the emotions leave your body and surrender the emotions. Let them go into the flames and into the words you are burning. Do as many purge letters as needed to help clear your negative emotions and to help you vibrate, as a human, as high as you possibly can.

SCAN THE QR CODE FOR THE PAST RELATIONSHIPS MEDITATION

9 Pink Bubble Healing

Choose to release anger and frustration, clearing away negative energy to keep your vibration high. Stay aligned with your beautiful, elevated energy and never lower it to match others.

How to use the pink bubble clearing:

Find a private place where no one can disturb you.

Ask God or the divine creator for a column of white light, all the way through you.

Visualise that you are standing in the column of white light.

Take some deep breaths and breath in the white light.

As you take a deep breath, the white light is collecting all the negative energy/anger or distractions you are feeling.

With your exhaling breath you are then going to breath out all the negative feelings into the imaginary pink balloon.

Blow all the breath in your lungs out of your mouth (like blowing up a balloon). Do this process a few times. Imagine or feel your pink balloon filling up with your negative feelings/anger/ frustration.

Once you feel like you have released into the balloon the negative energy you are feeling, ask Archangel Michael to convert the energy within the pink balloon to positive healing energy.

The balloon, now filled with positive energy can be sent back to yourself, or to the situation you are in or the room you are in, to help raise the vibration.

Before you leave the closed room, you are in, ask Archangel Michael for his beautiful blue cloak of protection, to help you stay safe and protected and in the light.

Thank God or the divine creator and Archangel Michael for his help today.

The pink bubble clearing is important to do every time you are feeling negative frustrations or anger. To live in the light and have a positive energy vibration, you cannot sit in anger and frustrations. It is important to clear out of your body the negative vibration. Especially when you are waiting to manifest your best life possible. This tool is great to use when your vibration has been lowered to clear negative energy from you.

**SCAN THE CODE FOR THE
PINK BUBBLE CLEARING MEDITATION**

10 Poverty Thoughts

This page is a reminder to become aware of your self-talk, especially around money and abundance. No successful person has a poverty mindset. It is time to reprogram your thinking to attract an abundant and fulfilling life.

People who are doing well in life, will have a positive mindset and a manifesting mindset. This page could also be to remind you to be around people who have a positive mindset and that are wanting to achieve similar goals to you and your family. If you want to soar like an eagle, you can't be flocking with the turkeys.

Some of my favourite affirmations are:

I'm always in the right place to attract positivity and abundance into my life.

In a perfect way, I can easily manifest _____ into my life by _____.

Another important reason to have a positive mindset is that you never want to give a poverty mindset to your children or family. If my kids want to do something that is not possible this week, because of the bills and out goings in expenses, I will always say, it's not in this week's budget, but let's add this to next weeks' goals, depending on what they are wanting. This is a great way to talk to your children or family because you reaffirm the positivity of money. It is also important to teach your children about budgeting and planning for the future. Just remember anyone can fly first class, but it may take you a bit longer to save the money for the airline ticket.

SCAN THE QR CODE FOR THE PURGING MEDITATION

11 Procrastination

*Stop procrastinating about a situation, plan
and start doing what is necessary.*

Avoiding situations is a horrible way to live. What a burden on your shoulders. Whether you have been procrastinating about your overdue tax return, decluttering your home, paying bills, or sorting paperwork; it is an unnecessary load to bear.

This feeling and burden on your shoulders, can be cleared by:

1. Writing a to do list.
2. Identifying small steps to help get started.
3. Everyday allot 20 minutes to help clear or start with the goal you want to achieve.
4. Ask a friend to help you get started or employ someone to assist you.

The main reason you have been drawn to this page is to start to release all the weighted energy of procrastination. It is time to live a life of ease. Our great God or the divine creator did not want us to constantly feel overwhelmed with life. Remember, Rome wasn't built in a day.

SCAN THE QR CODE FOR THE PURGING MEDITATION

12 Relationship Purge

*You have turned to this page to help
purge past relationships.*

This can be from your life so far. It can be friendships, work colleges, lovers, family relationships or any other relationships you've had with other humans. Do you often think of past lovers or friendships and have sadness that didn't end well? Sometimes this can be that both you and that person still think of each other, and a chord of your energy still resonates back and forth to each other. In your logical mind however, you know that it wasn't a good relationship to have in your life, so you've cut ties with them. It could also be that one of you didn't honour the spiritual contract that was organised before you came down from heaven and you're still a little heart broken by the breakup of the relationship.

The guides and angels are asking you to now let go of the negative emotions and face forward in your thinking to have the best, bright future possible. Archangel Michael is the Archangel to ask to help clear away all emotional baggage.

> Archangel Michael, I ask that you please clear away what no longer serves me, especially from old relationships, lovers, family, friends, work colleges and old school friends.

Take some deep breaths, as you are exhaling you are letting go of all the old negative emotions, Archangel Michael is clearing this energy from you.

You can do purge letters to this person and write down all your anger, frustration, hurt and sadness. Once you've written it, burn the letter and as it is burning let all the energy go into the fire. This is great to do on a full moon. On a new moon, write an intentions list on what you want in a new relationship, so you don't attract the same relationships over and over again.

SCAN THE QR CODE FOR THE PURGING MEDITATION

13 Positive Self Talk

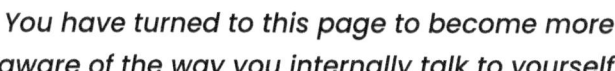

You have turned to this page to become more aware of the way you internally talk to yourself.

You are doing the best you can in life but let's change your internal dialogue with yourself. Have fun with yourself. The energy or vibration you give to others reflects how you think and talk to yourself. It is time to let go of the negative mind chatter and talk to yourself how you want others to talk to you. We are stuck with ourselves our whole lives, why not learn to like yourself and then love yourself. This starts with positive mind chatter to yourself.

To raise your vibration, your internal talk is very important. We want you to start talking to yourself like you are talking to your best friend. This is important when becoming the best version of yourself.

First, focus when you are doing daily jobs, not matter how ordinary or mundane. Congratulate yourself, "Great Job (say your name)!" There are lots of great ways to talk positively to yourself daily. Doing this all day will build up your vibration as well as your confidence within yourself. Whatever your dream goals are or your desires for this life, self-confidence is always needed. When you have negative thought about yourself, just say, "Cancel that thought". Positive self-talk takes time. They say a new habit takes 21 days to form, so be easy on yourself. Start to become consciously aware of how you are talking internally to yourself.

If you grew up in a home where your parents talked poorly to you, do the inner child healing meditation to help you heal. I always imagine Mother Mary to be a mother like figure. She will always talk positively and give you lots of encouragement.

Just remember, the positive saying lots of spiritual teachers say: Positive within, positive without. As within, as without. Being positive inside and out provides a great example to others and helps create a better more positive planet.

SCAN THE QR CODE FOR THE PAST RELATIONSHIPS MEDITATION

14 Shadow Self-Clearing

You have turned to this page to learn about your Shadow Self and how to clear negative vibrations.

We all have a dark side; it is something we can identify that we don't like about ourselves or a part of our personality. This can be within your soul from a past life or can be developed in your soul in this lifetime as a survival instinct from your childhood or throughout your life. Our shadow self can also be shown to us when you do not like something about someone, it is often mirroring an aspect of you, that you do not like. For your vibration to rise, you have to look at your whole soul and learn to clear your negative energies to raise your vibration.

Ways to help you identify your shadow self:

- What aspects of your personality come out when you are pushed or provoked in an argument?
- Are you judgmental, does your ego get in the way and sometimes you think you are better than others?
- Do you justify your self-worth by mentioning within your conversations, where you live or your job title etc?
- Does someone in your life really annoy you – have a think if it is a part of your personality that you don't like about you?
- Do you treat some people in your life poorly especially a lover or friends, this can be part of your shadow self?

How empathic and compassionate are we to others, do we judge them or are we trying to understand their situation they are in. I often see other people's lives like the movie Sliding doors, it is often one decision that placed them off path. Look at how you can help and support them not judge them for the situation they are in.

Your shadow self can also come up when you are around someone that has a life that you fear may happen to you. You don't like being around them because it is a fear you have about your own life. (This feeling can also come up when you are on social media, reading about someone's else's life and you want to delete your Facebook friend as its too confronting for you). Your shadow self may also come up in the form of jealousy, for example on social media when someone is achieving their goals, and you feel triggered that you are procrastinating and not achieving yours and you also want to delete the friend.

Shadow self-work can be confronting and make you feel uncomfortable in your own skin. Working on your shadow self can also be rewarding. This is helping you become the best soul possible while here on Earth, after all, the reason we came to Earth is to heal our soul and to evolve and learn our souls life lessons, this means all parts – the good, the bad and the ugly.

Take some time to use the shadow self meditation and to take note of your thoughts and how you interact with others. You will be so proud of yourself when you notice how your thoughts have become humbled and that your soul is equal to others regardless to what you have or own. We only walk into heaven with lessons learnt and experiences we have had.

SCAN THE QR CODE FOR THE SHADOW SELF MEDITATION

PART TWO

Motivational Messages

15 Abundance

Focus on all the abundance you already have and the abundance that is coming your way.

Have a look in your life now and begin to recognise what abundance you have acquired thus far; this will help create more abundance. The angels are trying to increase your abundance, but they also want you to focus on all the good you already have happening all around you. Looking at your life with lack, will cause you to have the opposite to abundance. Even if you drive an old car, look at the car with abundance, that it provides you the ability to go around town, to go to work and visit friends.

Momentum often starts small and then grows, this is the same with abundance. Abundance also grows when our emotions are rich and full of intention. To have your heart filled with an abundance of love for our family, does not cost us anything. Your family, however, will be enriched with your love for them, which is a very positive outcome.

The most successful people are the ones that see abundance in the small things in their life first. Be mindful today of all the abundance, you already have around you.

**SCAN THE QR CODE FOR
THE MANIFESTING MEDITATION**

16 Bucket List

Don't just live day to day, live your best life.

Can you write a list of all the things you want to do before your earthly time ends. Too many people who are living their final years have regrets about what they didn't do. Most of the time, humans get caught up in living day to day or living a life to impress others, doing what they should be doing. Life goes by so quickly.

Write your bucket list of places you want to go to, things you want to complete, goals you want to do or achieve. Things you want to buy. Perhaps even people you want to say sorry to. Start a little bank account called bucket list. Have the account set up so that you cannot transfer money out online, so you must go to the bank to withdraw your money. Even if it is a small amount, every week, it is a start and it is creating a vibration within you of excitement of living your best life.

17 Do It, Do it!

*Do the things you have always
dreamt of doing or becoming.*

Do all the things you have thought you wanted to do when you were younger, but in life as an adult you have lost hope or 'adulting' has gotten in the way. Don't let fear replace your dreams. Study that course! Look at what you must do to own that property, or the business you like. Change your career to something you are passionate about. Forgive and have strength within yourself to end a relationship that's not serving you.

> The angels who help guide me always ask me, 'Will your 90-year-old self regret not having a go at this?'

Do it – the angelic realms are here to support you and help you as much as possible.

Do it – consider what you will regret when you're an old person on the porch, reliving your life decisions. We want you to have a smile and chuckle at all the good things you have done.

18 Grace, Rise above it

You are an incredible human, who deserves the best.

Sometimes people can be mean and horrible for no reason.

Don't let these people get you down or change your dreams and goals.

Most of the time they are jealous and are living in their own fear.

The angels in the heavens, want you to **HAVE GRACE AND RISE ABOVE IT**.

Don't let anyone dull your sparkle and shine.

Most importantly, don't lower yourself to their bleak standards.

The angels are just reminding you to stay in your grace and integrity.

SCAN THE QR CODE FOR THE RAINBOW MEDITATION

19 Gratitude

Take a moment to slow down and appreciate the life you have. Stay present, embrace gratitude, and approach others with kindness and patience.

Think of 5-10 things you are grateful for, in your life.

> I'm grateful that I have drinkable water from my tap.
> I'm grateful for a flushing toilet.
> I'm grateful that I have warm clothes.
> I'm grateful I have food in my fridge to eat.
> I'm grateful for the warmth of the sun when I stand facing it.
> I'm grateful that I can read.

Be grateful for what you have, your energy vibration will rise and help you manifest and have the life you are truly wanting. There is always something to be grateful for in life.

**SCAN THE QR CODE FOR THE
LIVING WITH GRATITUDE MEDITATION**

20 Gut Instinct, Trust

Always go with your gut instincts and trust your feelings, intuition about a situation or person.

The angelic realm wants you to pay attention to and trust your gut instinct. The more you apply your instincts and realise they are correct, the more confidence you will have in yourself. Gut instinct or the knowing, as some people call it, is the best tool you have, to guide you toward the most amazing life. Trusting yourself and the decisions you make are, in most souls – soul lessons here on Earth.

If you have children, start to help your children learn to use their gut instinct. As a parent, this is one of the most important tools you can give your children and will help them to become happy and successful as an adult. If they don't want to go somewhere or do something because it doesn't feel right in their stomach, go with it.

If you have made some poor choices, you may want to seek guidance from Jo at www.joanneplater.com.au. In particular, the Purging Meditation will help you clear your mind and body of all the negative energy and thoughts about your past decisions.

SCAN THE QR CODE FOR THE PURGING MEDITATION

21 Look Forward

This page has been selected for you by the universe to remind you to look forward to your bright future.

So many of my clients are going through life, looking back at lost loves, broken friendships, and regrets. It is as though they are walking backwards toward their future. Where are your thoughts? Are you looking backwards to your past, or forward to your bright future?

Be conscious of what you are thinking about. What you think about the most is what we become; we want to create the best future possible. We cannot change our past, but we can think positively to create the best bright future possible. Spend the next week being conscious of where your thoughts go. Aim to think in the now as often as you can. Do great things today to create a better tomorrow. Remember your future self will thank you.

22 Lovers

Open your heart to love, whether inviting a new partner into your life or nurturing positive change in your existing relationship.

Are you clear with what you want in your next lover? Are you thinking in a positive way about what you want? All intentions should start with a positive. The universe is responsive to your intentions and your words as well as with the energy you are feeling. Even thinking or writing in the negative can inadvertently attract that energy. For example, if you were to write down, I don't want a person who is narcissistic. Guess what you are going to attract? Instead write what you do want. I want a person whose fun loving and kind to all. All intentions are to be written in the positive. Even when you are going on a date focus on the positive in the future not what you attracted in the past.

If you are focusing on a current relationship, be it with your lover, life partner, husband, wife or even business partner, there is a few things to keep in mind. The relationship is worth saving and just needs a few things to change. If there is ongoing conflict or frustrations, first see if it may be something you are doing to make your partner react the way they are. Most importantly, use positive forms of communication to gently work though the relationship, listening and voicing your opinions to create a positive change for both people. Create boundaries to help everyone feel heard and their needs met and daily check in with yourself and each other to keep on track.

SCAN THE CODE FOR LETTING GO OF SOULMATES AND TWIN SOULS

23 Manifesting

Now is the time to manifest your best life.

Now is the time to manifest what you really want in your life. If you were to ask 10 successful people how they made it, 9 out of 10 will say it happened with a positive mindset and a vision of what they wanted to manifest. They had laser like focus of what they wanted. Where you place your thoughts is where you will get your results. Start today, write a list of what you are wanting in life. Some of the ways to help manifest is a vision board that you see 2-3 times a day. On the way to the toilet or in your bedroom, on a board in your kitchen. By looking at your goals 2-3 times a day, keeps you focused on what you are wanting to achieve. Another way is to write down your goals and laminate them and place them in your toilet, in your shower, on your bedside table so you read them before you go to sleep and when you wake up. In the car, have a little symbol that represents your goal to remind you to keep focused. (For example, a little monopoly house if you as saving for a home.)

I suggest writing the following and reading often:

- I can easily achieve _____.

- I can easily achieve _____.

In a perfect way, I will be able to save $_____ by month and year.

I'm in the right place at the right time to attract abundance and goodness into my life.

Your energy and belief must match what you are wanting to manifest. Be grateful for every single good thing that happens in your life, no matter how small. This positive thinking encourages the positive mindset to begin to vibrate higher, to achieve what you are wanting in your life. We should aim every day to 'give it our best shot' and create the life we want.

SCAN THE QR CODE FOR A MANIFESTING MEDITATION TO CLEAR BLOCKAGES AND HELP YOU DEFINE AND ATTRACT YOUR GOALS

24 Wealth

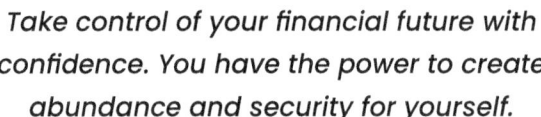

Take control of your financial future with confidence. You have the power to create abundance and security for yourself.

I'm always in the right place to attract abundance in all areas of my life. The best way to attract more money is to know how exactly much you need to generate to have an amazing life. Ask any successful person, they will know precisely what they need to generate per month or per week, to have the life they are living. The angels and universe want you to be prosperous, but they cannot help people who are ostriches that bury their head in the sand and hope for the best. Have a look at your expenses and work out where some changes can be made, how you can spend less and save more. Write a list of what your financial intentions are and what you want to achieve in 3 months, 6 months and 1 year. Slow and steady intentions are a great way to attract all the money you need. Remember, it's not the brand of handbag or wallet that matters, it is what's inside your wallet, that shows your real intentions and your real success. The angelic realm find it easier to help someone with clear goals and intentions then someone that has no idea what you are needing.

25 Surrender

By turning to this page, you are being guided to surrender and release any negative emotions and baggage you are carrying.

The purpose of surrendering and releasing is for your soul's journey, enabling you to better your own human experience. It is not for the person who has done wrong by you.

Let go of any negative feelings, or the trauma caused by the way someone did or didn't treat you or look after you. Surrender the emotions connected to a situation that did not go well for you. Surrendering and releasing will help your energy grow to have a happier and more joyful life. This experience will also give you permission to be in-charge of your happiness. Do not allow your situation, a person or an event have control over your happiness. Now's the time to surrender and release the situation, person or your past to have your best life possible.

Suggestions on ways to release:

- Purge/surrender letters to the person or situation and then burn the letters.
- Throw rocks in the ocean and swear, cry, scream out the situation.
- Meditations – there are 3 great meditations on joanneplater.com.au to help purge and increase your energy and create a positive outlook.
- Focus on where your thoughts are. Are your thoughts always in the past – thinking over and being in the shoulda, coulda, woulda? Your thoughts need to be in the present moment and

thinking about your bright future. Try to be mindful of this and thinking in the moment.
- Sometimes, sending a pretend email or text to the person may help. However, Do Not Send it to the person. The exercise is to let all your anger and frustration out and to surrender and release to the situation from your mind, body and soul.

PART THREE

Body

26 Detox

Have you been overindulging in processed foods and alcohol and soft drinks, using toxic products or recreational drugs?

The angels are asking you if you can make some changes to your lifestyle. They want you to have the best earthly experience, to do this they want you to look after your body. Begin to make small changes and you will start to feel less sluggish and have more energy. Adding more vegetables and fresh fruit to your daily eating. Choosing healthy options to have more life force. Have you been drinking 8 glasses of filtered water? Are you getting enough sleep? Sometimes it's also good to have a think about who you are spending time with. Are they a bad influence on your daily habits? Have you been emotionally eating?

Let's ask Archangel Michael to help clear the worry and emotions from your body to help you lessen your emotional eating and drinking or usage of recreational drugs.

> Archangel Michael, please help me clear all overlaid emotional energy from my chakras and emotional body and to help me to be stronger within myself to choose a healthier lifestyle.

SCAN THE QR CODE FOR A CHAKRA BALANCE MEDITATION

This meditation will support you in making positive changes and living a more cleansed life physically, mentally and emotionally.

27 Detox Technology

We did not come to have an earth soul experience only to be stuck on our devices, our phone, iPad, PC, laptops, or TV.

We came here to experience earths great gifts; the wind on our face, the smell of the air at the beach, to be in an amazing crowd of people at a concert, to walk through a museum and get goose bumps over our body at the beauty of the art works. The universe is asking you to engage in Mother Nature, go outside and enjoy Mother Nature. Notice and smell the grass, the flowers, and trees and spend time with your bare feet on the grass. Go for a swim in the ocean or lake, emerge yourself in the beauty of floating in the water with sun on your face. Talk to your friends, your family and community in person instead of merely sending a text. Get some real Face to Face time. If you are feeling lonely or isolated, could it be because you are not engaging with people in person? Humans are social, we need human interactions and human touch. We also long for the connective touch with Mother Earth. Schedule time for immersing yourself in Mother Nature, you'll feel so much better. Even if it is just on your lunch break. Make the effort to go outside of your office, sit on a park bench and eat your lunch in the sun with your feet on the grass. I bet you will be so much more productive in the afternoon than sitting at your desks through your lunch break. Find a walking group or social team to play some sport in.

The angelic realm is asking you to engage more with humans and Mother Earth.

28 Protection

This page will show you how to protect your energy from others.

Do you ever feel drained or flat in energy after talking to someone or being around a person or place? This protection is great to do every morning when you get up. I suggest you anchor it to something you do every morning, so perhaps when you are washing your hands after you go to the toilet. Archangel Michael loves helping people protect their energy.

> Ask God or the Divine creator for a column of white light all around you.
> Ask Archangel Michael to clear all other people's energy from you.
> Ask Archangel Michael to clear away any ill wishes, jealous energy, or any other negative energy you may have attached to you. Take some deep breaths and allow Archangel Michael to clear this for you.
> Ask Archangel Michael for his blue cloak of protections or blue shield of protection around you.

If you know the person who is draining in your life, you can also ask God or the Divine Creator for a column of white light between you and the person. This will prevent them from drawing on your energy and they will take God or the Divine creator's energy instead.

You will see a big difference in your energies and will feel amazing if you can do this daily.

29 Rest and Recover

*It is time to pause and rest. To take time out
to relax and recover from your busy life.*

By taking some time off to fill up your tank, you will be so much more energetic and to be able to think clearly and physically do more. Most people have a soul lesson to learn, one which can be very challenging. It is how to maintain balance in their lives. Sometimes having a week off every 9 weeks can help you feel rejuvenated or sometimes daily meditation will help you stay clear minded and focused on your goals and tasks. Relaxing at home and having a staycation, with reading, watching a movie or going for walks can help you to reset and relax. Our journey here on Earth is so quick, it's time to start to enjoy the feeling of the wind in your face, to watch a sunrise or sunset often, to breath in forest air. To have a great belly laugh moment with friends and family or while watching a comedy.

Start to live your life, for all the moments you can't buy but only enjoy.

30 Water

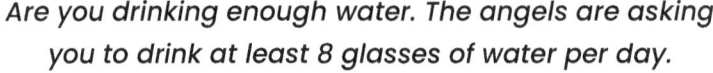

Are you drinking enough water. The angels are asking you to drink at least 8 glasses of water per day.

This does not include tea, coffee, or soft drink. Fresh, filtered water where possible, and not in a plastic container – glass or a tin is better as studies have shown the chemicals from the plastic can leach into your water. If the health of your body is suffering from constipation, headaches, your skin is dry, you feel sluggish and have brain fog or even with anxiety; there is sometimes a link that your body is needing more water. You can have herbal tea, water with lemon or fresh ginger or a slice of orange or lime, if you don't like the taste of water. Beautiful, fresh, filtered water is key. Your organs, brain and skin will be so thankful. Your whole wellbeing will change for the better when you drink more water each day.

Most people reading this will be living in a 1st world country, yet most are dehydrated like they live in a 3rd world country. This is by our unconscious decisions or not living and feeling what our body is needing.

Make a conscious decision to stay hydrated.

PART FOUR

Magic and Mystery

31 Celebrations

It is time to celebrate your life journey so far. You have started the work on becoming the best person you can be, and it is now time to celebrate you.

You are a good person, and the angelic realm are here with you to celebrate you. Be proud of how far you have come. Take time to reflection on how much you have grown and how you are becoming a better person. Be kind and loving to yourself, you have grown so much. Celebrate the beautiful soul you are becoming. God or the Divine creator, or your spirit guides are all here to love and support you. More good things are coming into your life. Celebrate the small and the large wins in your life. Celebrate with a grateful heart and take time to love this moment madly. Know the angels want you to have many celebrations in your life. Smile, good moments are coming your way.

32 Divine Timing

Trust in divine timing, everything unfolds for your highest good at the perfect moment.

The angelic guides always want us to give our lives the best shot! However, what we want and when we want it may not be in our best interest. If you are trying start a relationship but the timing is off, set it free. If they stay or come back, it is meant to be. Sometimes you just need to relax and have faith. If you have been trying for a promotion but it's been given to someone else, sit for a moment and ask if that is what you are truly wanting. In my 20's I desperately wanted a promotion being offered at my workplace. I did not get it and so I applied for another job entirely. I got that job which turned out to be much better working conditions and came with a massive pay rise.

Have faith, that all that happens is within a plan for something better for you. The angels are just wanting you to take note. What comes easily in your life and what feels like a hand brake is on, there is usually a reason for both.

33 Goals and Dreams

If you are looking for a universal sign.
THIS IS YOUR SIGN.

Keep going, you are just getting started. Your magnificent self and the greatness that you have has only been seen by others so slightly. Step into the confidence the angels are sending you to feel self-assured and walk in the direction to achieve your goals and dreams. You have so much more light and goodness to show and give the world. The angels are sending you love, thanks, support and extra energy to help you achieve more of your dreams and goals. Make sure, you keep a to-do list. At least every week, do something to help you achieve your goals. Remember also to look after yourself and your health, to help you keep on track.

SCAN THE QR CODE FOR THE LETTING GO OF FEAR AND DOUBT MEDITATION

34 Power

You are stepping into your power, embracing your best self, and aligning with your soul's path. Take time to envision and feel what you truly want to achieve.

When you are on the journey to your soul's purpose, you will experience and feel a power within you that seems unstoppable with your passion and path for this lifetime. The angels want you to know that they are all around you to help you be powerful and follow your soul's purpose. Be the powerful soul you are meant to be. Empowerment starts within you, once you start making changes the angelic realms can help you and support you.

35 Signs

*The angels are guiding you through signs,
reassuring you that you are on the right path.
A white butterfly, a familiar scent, or other gentle
reminders may be messages from loved ones who
have passed, letting you know they are with you.*

I love watching or noticing signs in my life. Some people will notice signs on number plates on cars or songs playing on the radio. Believe, there is no such thing as coincidences. Signs are there or here for us to know that there is a spiritual world around us, consisting of passed over relatives, and our own spiritual guides and angels who are helping us, here on Earth.

Some other examples of signs are seeing the same numbers repeatedly. It could be seeing a rainbow. I often smell roses when Archangel Mary or Mother Mary come into my healing room to help a client, I'm with. Watch for signs in your life, they are all around you. The angels and guides are always wanting to connect with you.

PART FIVE

Your Team

36 Dragons

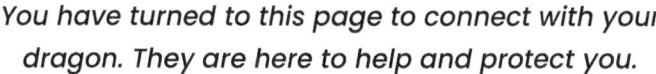

You have turned to this page to connect with your dragon. They are here to help and protect you.

In 2012, many thousands of dragons came to Earth to help elevate the energy here. I connected to my dragon during this time, and he has now helped me in so many ways. They love you unconditionally and want you to have the best life here on Earth.

In meditation or quiet time away from all the distractions, perhaps sitting in mother nature, you can connect with your dragon. They can be large or small, silver, white, purple – whatever you see or whatever you feel, this is what your dragon looks like. The dragons can help clear away negative energy and clear a path of positive energy ahead of you to help you feel safe and protected here on Earth. They help you attract abundance into your life whether it be personal or for your job or a business that you own. They can also use their energy to clean within your home or workspace.

You can also ask your dragon to clear away negative energy and overlaid energy from other humans. For example, you may have had a good conversation with someone, yet afterwards you have felt tired or overwhelmed or can't stop thinking about them; you can ask your dragon to clear their energy from you.

You can do this by saying:

> 'My personal dragon, can I ask you to clear away the negative energy from (say their name), please clear all chords and attachments from me.'

Your dragon is here to help your raise the energy surrounding you, or a particular situation, and they love helping. If there is an area or place that has been in conflict or has a negative feel to it, you can ask your dragon to clear the space. If this area is owned by someone, you would have to ask for their permission to clear the space. Your dragon especially loves to help you have the best day. Please ask your dragon to send their energy ahead of you, keeping you safe and protected and to keep the energy high and clear for you to stay positively charged, all day long. Make it a goal to get to know your personal dragon, they love you unconditionally. Talk to them as often as possible to help build a relationship with them.

The dragons are here to connect to each person individually but are also here to help raise the vibration of the planet. By asking to clear your energy or a place that needs more energy, you are helping to raise the vibration higher.

SCAN THE QR CODE FOR A MEDITATION GETTING TO KNOW YOUR PERSONAL DRAGON

37 The Elementals

Now is the time to connect with your elementals. They are all around us. They are our Mother Nature, encouraging you to notice your spiritual signs in your life.

Elementals help ground us; to allow us to come back into the body and be here in the now and enjoy the moment we are in. How often do we go to the beach and feel better about our lives? That is the work of the Undines, the water elementals. The calm of the ebb and flow, the sparkling of the waters, the cleansing energy, all of this is the water elementals.

When we take time to relax in front of a fire to ponder life, it's the fire elementals, the Salamanders. A calmness ignites within us a feeling of contentment, and all is well in the world. Breathing in fresh air is the Sylphs elementals. Taking a deep breath is so healing and can change our state instantly. It allows us to see hope and to rejuvenate our energy. The Sylphs also create wind, how beautiful it is to feel the wind on our face. Fairies and gnomes in our gardens and in mother nature, are here to help lift our vibration as a human. They are also here to help lift our human hearts to see the beauty and wonder in our world. In doing this, we will help the Earth vibrate at a higher level and bring more gratitude into your surroundings.

Take note of all the beautiful things you can see when you take the time in mother nature. Ocean or river swimming, forest bathing, walking in mother nature, strolling the sunlit shores, and walking in the silence of the snow. Simply sitting in your garden at home and watching the birds and butterflies, all in perfect harmony. Take note of what signs the elementals are giving you. Butterflies, dragonflies or even a type of bird may signify something special to you. Find the beauty in nature as the elementals are in nature all around you.

You can also connect with all the elements while meditating, especially the fairies and gnomes. You may have different fairies and gnomes, or the same fairies and gnomes you connect with every day.

Journal your experiences with the elemental kingdom, you'll be surprised how much they want us to connect with them.

SCAN THE QR CODE TO CONNECT WITH YOUR ELEMENTALS, UNICORNS, AND DRAGONS

38 Meeting your Spirit Guide

You have turned to this page to start a relationship with your spirit guides.

When we come to Earth, we are assigned a guardian angel, our spirit guide. They are here to love you and to help you have a spiritually connected and abundant life on Earth. Your spirit guide who has been assigned only to you; will help you try to learn all your lessons you're wanting to learn while you are here. They will guide you toward your soul's purpose. These lessons were discussed before you came to Earth with your spiritual family in heaven.

Your spirit guide is a soul who has learnt all the lessons on Earth, and who has evolved and elevated to a spirit guide in the heavens. The beautiful thing is that they have chosen you to help you evolve here on Earth in your lifetime, the lifetime you're in right now. They are not a family member who has passed; however, these souls will be around you as well.

Spirit guides are with you to love you unconditionally, to be your best friend, your support angel and will do their best to help you have the best life. Through meditation you can connect with your spirit guide. The more you can meditate the better the connection. It's like any relationship, the time you spent together – the better the relationship.

To start with you may see energy or feel your spirit guide around you. This may be how you connect with your spirit guide. After some time, you may start to see their face, hear their voice, or get a very strong sense of their presence around you.

Your spirit guide doesn't change as you evolve, your spirit guide will stay the same. Of course, other guides may join you from time to time throughout your life. Some spirit guides you have had past lives with, and they have evolved to help us in this life. In such cases, you may feel a familiar energy around your spirit guides.

SCAN THE QR CODE FOR A MEDITATION TO HELP YOU CONNECT WITH YOUR SPIRIT GUIDE

39 Unicorns

You have turned to this page to open your mind and connect with your personal unicorn.

As with the dragons, in 2012 many thousands of unicorns came to Earth to help increase the frequency and vibration on planet Earth. Your personal unicorn is standing next to you now. Your unicorn wants to introduce themselves to you. Your unicorn is here to help lift the energy of your body and to raise your vibrational energy to help you be able to manifest your best life. Earth's vibration and the frequency of Earth will rise when you work with your unicorn. Ask them to help you rise and achieve your goals and dreams, it is a ripple effect of good vibrations. Your unicorn is also here to help you clear away negative energy from your chakra system. This can help you achieve your dreams and goals as there is fewer negative blocks within your chakra system. To do this you can ask your unicorn to touch each of your chakras with their golden horn to help clear any negative energy or any emotional blocks you may have to achieve your dream.

Example would be:

> 'My unicorn, help me clear away any negative blocks in my chakra system that is holding me back from achieving (say the goal).'

The unicorn is going to touch their golden horn your base, sacral, solar plexus, heart, throat, third eye and crown chakra. You can also ask your unicorn to help give you extra energy if you have a busy day ahead, if you are not feeling well and need to help heal yourself, or if you've had a terrible night sleep and need some extra energy. Your unicorn is so happy to help, you just need to ask. Your unicorn can also spread their golden energy around your home to help raise the vibration of your home. The unicorns live in the heavens with Mother Mary and can not only help you connect to Mother Mary, but also to spread the energy of Motherly love over you. If your mother has passed or if you don't have a great relationship with your mother, ask the unicorns to wash over you the beautiful motherly energy from Mother Mary.

SCAN THE QR CODE FOR A MEDITATION TO HELP YOU CONNECT WITH YOUR UNICORN, DRAGON, AND ELEMENTALS

40 Heavenly Family Member

A heavenly family member wants to connect with you and remind you that you are supported and loved. This page is a symbol of their message: I love you.

Passed-over family members always want you to know that they are here to help you. Even if you had a strained relationship or did not know them well, they are still here to help and support you.

Take a moment, take some deep breaths, and see if a passed-over family member comes to your mind. They are often the one who is around you in this moment. You may smell their familiar scent or notice a particular sound or symbol that relates to them, either today or in the next few days.

They are sending love to you.

If you had a challenging relationship with someone while they were alive, you can still heal the relationship. You can do this while meditating, talking to them as you walk along the beach or through beautiful bushland, or writing them a letter to release the emotions you are feeling. This includes expressing any anger or sadness towards them. The passed-over family member will be more than happy to help clear away karma between the two of you.

41 Universal Healing

The Universal Healing Council is asking you to send their healing energy to a situation in your life that needs healing or to a situation happening here on Earth.

The Universal Healing Council is asking you to be a part of their council and to ground their universal healing energy into the Earth. They ask you to then send this energy to a country or situation that needs healing, to lift the vibration in an area, or to support a family member or someone in your community. Instead of feeling worried, angry or pitying someone in a difficult situation, ask the universal healers to assist you. You can ask for a column of white light around you. Then, ask for the universal healing energy to surround you, and in your third eye – your mind's eye, visualise yourself sending energy to the person, people or situation. Throughout the day, you can continue sending universal healing energy to the person or situation.

PART SIX

Chakra Healing

42 Base Chakra

You have turned to this page to learn and understand your base chakra or to help you unblock your energy within your base chakra.

The base chakra is located at the base of your spine.

The chakra vibrates to the colour of red.

This chakra is developed between the ages of 0-7 years of age.

The base chakra physically includes your hip, feet legs, base of the spine, bladder, and prostate.

It's the first part of our physical structure that is created in the womb, so it's a great chakra to start to learn about. Our base chakra is the chakra to help us feel grounded here on Earth, its where our sense of belief is within us. Your fight and flight response are developed in the base chakra. Also, within the base chakra our sense of belonging, integrity, and self-esteem. This is all the emotions we need for our survival. We even learn to eat and drink at the development of this chakra.

When your base chakra is balanced you will feel vitalised and excited about life. You feel centred in your life, you feel financially secure in the way you earn money, you feel connected to nature, you feel safe and secure in your environment, you feel confident and adapt to your life changing.

When your base chakra is unbalanced, you will be afraid and worry that your basic needs won't be met, you are always worried about your survival e.g., how will you eat this week, I hope I have a secure place to sleep and rest. You always feel ungrounded and scattered in your thoughts, you are unable to trust the universe that your needs will be met because of your fear of survival, this can lead to eating issues as an adult and your family will have contributed to your fear of survival from their fear of survival.

Physically to help balance your base chakra – dance in whatever way makes you happy, walk in nature, forest bathing, swim in the ocean or river, dance in the rain, do yoga or an exercise classes, have a beautiful bath with Epsom or deep-sea mineral salts and/or essential oils in your bath.

Foods to help your base chakra are all red foods – apples, beans, raspberries, tomatoes, strawberries, cherries, pomegranates, peppers, radishes, beets, watermelons.

Affirmations to say to help clear your base chakra
  I am grounded, secure, and safe.
  I belong in this world.
  I have all that I need.

Crystals to help elevate your vibration in your base chakra are red jasper, red garnet, red carnelian, hematite, smokey quartz, blood stone, ruby, red tigers' eye, and black tourmaline.

The essential oils to help the base chakra are ginger, sandalwood, myrrh, cedarwood, vetiver, patchouli, and rosewood.

The yoga poses to help the base chakra are warrior 1, the tree pose.

BELOW IS A QR CODE TO A MEDITATION
TO HELP YOU CLEAR AND INCREASE YOUR
VIBRATION IN YOUR BASE CHAKRA

43 Sacral Chakra

You have turned to this page to learn and understand your sacral chakra or to help you unblock your energy within your sacral chakra.

The sacral chakra is located just below your navel.

The chakra vibrates to the colour of orange.

This chakra is developed between the ages of 7–14 years of age.

The sacral chakra physically includes your reproductive system (ovaries or testicles) hips, bladder, and lower back.

The sacral chakra is our connection to our emotional, creative and our sexual expression. The way we connect to relationships with other humans and the relationships and feelings associated with money are all within our sacral chakra.

When your sacral chakra is balanced you will feel energetic and inspired in life, you are able to freely express your creative side – you can voice your pleasures and enjoy being intimate. You live your life with grace, flow and flexibility and can adapt to situations easily that arise on your soul's journey on Earth. You have compassion and forgiveness to yourself and others.

When your sacral chakra is unbalanced, you have feelings of guilt and can be jealous of others, you have a low sex drive or are confused about your sexuality, you have issues with enjoying being intimate and feeling pleasure. Creatively you may feel blocked or feel you are not creative at all. You can be controlling in situations and have issues with trying to be or feel in power. Financially you will have a poor relationship with money either overspending or avoiding your financial situation, you may also block prosperity coming into your life.

Physically to help balance your sacral chakra, try being around or in water or anything associated with water – spending time by the ocean, lake, river, or waterfalls. Drinking fresh clean water. Being creative, especially around water or association with water.

Foods to help the sacral chakra are all orange foods – oranges, carrots, rock melons, almonds, passion fruits, coconuts, mandarins, mangoes, walnuts, and papayas.

Affirmations to say
I possess the ability, power, and knowledge to create.
My emotions flow freely and I'm emotionally balanced.
I honour my sensuality, and I value my relationships with myself and others.

Crystals to help the sacral chakra are jasper, carnelian, citrine, amber, tigers' eye, mookate, goldstone, calcite, and sunstone.

The essential oils to help the sacral chakra are clary sage, neroli, orange, sandalwood, bergamot, geraniums, jasmine and rose.

The yoga poses to help the sacral charka are butterfly pose, shiva pose, the triangle pose and cobra pose.

BELOW IS A QR CODE TO A MEDITATION
TO HELP YOU CLEAR AND INCREASE YOUR
VIBRATION IN YOUR SACRAL CHAKRA

44 Solar Plexus Chakra

You have turned to this page to learn and understand your solar plexus chakra or to help you unblock your energy within your solar plexus chakra.

The solar plexus chakra is located just in your stomach area.

The chakra vibrates to the colour of yellow.

This chakra is developed between the ages of 14–21 years of age.

The solar plexus chakra physically includes your stomach, mid back, rib cage, liver, pancreas, digestive system, and bowels.

The solar plexus is our connection to our emotional sense of self. How we feel about ourselves and what we believe others think of us, our self-esteem being low or high in ego. This is greatly determined by how our parents treated us, if they helped you grow as a soul – you would feel more confident and have a feeling of being secure about who you are. If your parents were controlling, you will seek others for self-assurance and self-acceptance.

When your solar plexus chakra is balanced you have feelings of harmony and that you are safe and protected in your life. You are happy within yourself and accept others as they are. You have a great sense of purpose and can easily set goals and have great self-esteem. You have boundaries in place with family, work and friendships and can easily say "No", if what they are asking does not align with your core values or your goals for your life. You know when to be assertive and have a great level of self-confidence.

When your solar plexus chakra is unbalanced, you have low self-esteem and feelings of inadequacy, you set unrealistic goals that are often to impress others and have materialistic centred goals. You have lots of ideas of goals and a definition of success to impress others and to keep up with others who you find impressive. You often depend too much on the opinion of others, relying on this to feel good about yourself, which can lead to mood swings.

Physically to help balance your solar plexus, bath in sunlight especially your stomach area and allow more sunlight into your home. Spend some time around a campfire, bonfire or gazing at a fireplace. Have lovely candles around to see and feel their presence in your home.

Foods to help the solar plexus are all yellow foods – corn, pineapple, squash, beans, peppers/capsicum, bananas, lemons, brown rice, oats, millet, quinoa, amaranth, spices of ginger and turmeric.

Affirmations to say
I can honour the power within me.
I make my own decisions with confidence and conviction.
I give myself permission to be my authentic self.
I am worthy and empowered. I am motivated and proactive.

Crystals to help solar plexus topaz, citrine, yellow ziccon, amber, tigers' eye, yellow jasper, yellow sapphire, yellow tourmaline, pyrite, moonstone, golden labradorite, sunstone, agraginite.

The essential oils to help the solar plexus are lemon verbena, lemongrass, citronella, aniseed, ginger, juniper, rosemary, peppermint, pine, grapefruit, chamomile, rosewood, lime, fennel, coriander, and myrrh.

The yoga poses to help the solar plexus are cat/cow, sun salutation, bow pose and the cobra pose.

BELOW IS A QR CODE TO A MEDITATION TO HELP YOU CLEAR AND INCREASE YOUR VIBRATION IN YOUR SOLAR PLEXUS CHAKRA

45 Heart Chakra

You have turned to this page to learn and understand your heart chakra or to help you unblock your energy within your heart chakra.

The heart chakra is in the centre of your chest area.

The chakra vibrates to the colour of green.

This chakra is developed between the ages of 21–28 years of age.

The heart chakra physically includes your heart and cardio-vascular system, lungs, arms, shoulder blades and hands.

The heart chakra emotionally represents love, acceptance, and compassion. The heart chakra is the bridge between the body and the mind.

When your heart chakra is balanced you have a divine love for yourself and others, you can embrace compassion, you are able to forgive and accept and be understanding to others, you have feelings of contentment and are at peace with your life.

When your heart chakra is unbalanced, you are disconnected from yourself and others. You often feel lonely, even in a room full of people and often feel alienated from others. When given or shown love, you don't feel worthy. You are out of touch with who you are or who you want to be. You often can feel emotionally unstable and have bouts of very low depressive moods, mood swings and a heaviness in your heart chakra.

Physically to help balance your heart chakra spend time outside in the wind, feeling it blow through you. Flying a kite and blowing away all your heartaches and worries. Driving with the windows down. Practising deep breathing especially outside helps you to balance your heart chakra. Volunteering to help others and spending time with people you love and that love you. Loving an animal.

Foods to help your heart chakra are kale, kiwi fruit, cabbage, broccoli, lettuce, celery, green peppers/capsicums, zucchinis, pears, green apples, grapes, avocadoes, cucumbers, spinach, and plums.

Affirmations to say
   I allow myself to love.
   I forgive myself as well as those who have hurt me.
   I am worthy of healthy, unconditional love.
   I accept myself and love myself more every day.

Crystals to help are rose quartz, emeralds, green jade, tourmaline, malachite.

The essential oils to help your heart chakra are ylang ylang, rose, jasmine, vetiver, geranium, pine, rosewood, blue chamomile.

The yoga poses heart opening poses, cobra pose, cat/cow, upward facing dog.

BELOW IS A QR CODE TO A MEDITATION
TO HELP YOU CLEAR AND INCREASE YOUR
VIBRATION IN YOUR HEART CHAKRA

46 Throat Chakra

You have turned to this page to learn and understand your throat chakra or to help you unblock your energy within your throat chakra.

The throat chakra is in the throat area.

The chakra vibrates to the colour of blue.

This chakra is developed between the ages of 28–35.

The throat chakra physically includes the thyroid gland, throat, arms, digestive track, back of the neck area, nose, voice box, tongue, mouth, ears, cervical spine.

The throat chakra is our connection to the emotional expression of our feelings. If the throat is unbalanced, it will disconnect your heart and crown chakra. It is our truth and communication, our self-expression area. Our throat chakra expresses our creativity and purpose in life.

When your throat chakra is balanced you can easily speak your truth. You feel confident around close friends and family to speak your truth or your opinions. You can easily express your feelings by journaling or writing a letter or email to friends. You are happy to sing along with friends and family and belt out a good tune while you are in the shower. You rarely suffer from health ailments like a stiff neck, sore throat or thyroid issues.

When your throat chakra is unbalanced, you have lack of control over your speech whether you over talk or not express your thoughts and feelings enough. You can be a poor listener, can have excessive fear of speaking and difficulty expressing your truth. You can also over share, lie or embellish the truth. Thyroid issues and feelings of anxiety can also happen when you feel you can't express your thoughts, feelings and are able to express your creativity. You can suffer from sore throats when not speaking your truth or feel you are unable to speak your truth. If you are inflexible with your view point you are expressing or chatting to others, you can get a stiff neck.

Physically to help balance your throat, sing! Purge your emotions by yelling in an appropriate area like a deserted beach, write your thought and feelings in your journal or a purge letter to the person you feel your cant share your true feelings with.

Foods to help your throat are blueberries, apples, apricots, plums, pears, peaches, lemons, lime, and herbal chamomile tea.

Affirmations to say
I am aware and speak my truth.
I speak clearly, truthfully, and powerfully.
I am honest and authentic in my speech and actions.

Crystals to help the throat chakra are sodalite, amazonite, aquamarine, blue quartz, blue howelite, blue tiger's eye, blue apatite, lapis lazuli. Labradorite, turquoise, blue lace agate and blue apatite.

The essential oils to help the throat chakra rosemary, lime, cedarwood, sage, basil, chamomile, lemon, spearmint, tea tree, cypress, eucalyptus, ylang ylang, peppermint

The yoga poses to help the throat chakra are camel, plough, bridge, fish, standing forward bend, bow.

BELOW IS A QR CODE TO A MEDITATION
TO HELP YOU CLEAR AND INCREASE YOUR
VIBRATION IN YOUR THROAT CHAKRA

47 Third Eye Chakra

You have turned to this page to learn and understand your third eye chakra or to help you unblock your energy within your sacral chakra.

The third eye chakra is located in between your eyes.

The chakra vibrates to the colour of indigo blue.

This chakra is developed between the ages of 35–42.

The third eye chakra physically includes your eyes, nose, brain, ears, nervous system, and pineal glands.

The third eye chakra emotionally helps you have good judgement about others, you will have a great ability to see what's happening in a situation without over reactivating. Your imagination and creative abilities will be great when your third eyes balanced emotionally.

When your third eye chakra is balanced you have great intuition and a clairvoyant eye. You have psychic powers and start to connect to your higher self. You will experience more clairvoyant visions which happen when you are meditating or in your dreams. Within your third eye you will have a great vision for your wellbeing and future. You will have a clarity on direction of your life.

When your third eye chakra is unbalanced, you can have an overactive third eye. This means you can have unrealistic fantasies and ideas. Your view on your life can be an illusion to what your life is really like. You can create catastrophe in your life and over worry about what's happening in your life. If your third eye has an energetic block you may find your intuition blocked and find it hard to see intuitive visions and meditate.

Physically to help balance your third eye, outside in the light and gazing into the sun light, meditating outside or inside with natural light streaming onto your face, have a break from blue screens e.g., phones, tv, screens. Having good amount of sleep also helps your third eye.

Foods to help your third eye are blueberries, egg plant, prunes, grapes, figs, purple carrots, and purple cabbage.

Affirmations to say
I am connected to my highest intuition and highest truth.
I think clearly and only see the truth.
I trust my inner knowing and intuition.

Crystals to help to help your third eye Lapis Lazuli, amethyst, purple fluorite, sodalite, tanzanite, dumortierite, Iolite.

The essential oils clary sage, lavender, sandalwood, frankincense, pine, thyme, and vanilla.

The yoga poses to help your third eye are child's pose, warrior III, eagle pose.

BELOW IS A QR CODE TO A MEDITATION
TO HELP YOU CLEAR AND INCREASE YOUR
VIBRATION IN YOUR THIRD EYE CHAKRA

48 Crown Chakra

You have turned to this page to learn and understand your crown chakra or to help you unblock your energy within your crown chakra.

The crown chakra is located at the top of your head.

The chakra vibrates to the colour of soft lavender/purple.

This chakra is developed between the ages of 42–49.

The crown chakra physically includes the top of your head, brain, nervous system, lymphatic system, and hair.

The crown chakra is our connection to our emotional inner wisdom and having clarity to make the best decisions for our life. It is our connection to our spiritual wisdom and our acceptance of ourselves. It is directly related to our focus and determination in life.

When your crown chakra is balanced you will have a strong faith that the universe will look after you and provide for you. You have a connection that love is all around you. You understand what life is like here on Earth and that you are here to learn soul lessons. You have an enormous understanding, focus and determination for your goals and dreams. You often can find the good in others and have gratitude in all that you have.

When your crown chakra is unbalanced you can feel very lonely here on Earth, wondering aimlessly through your life. You have a lack of spiritual connection. Depression can happen often or low mood levels and times of feeling hopeless. You overthink experiences in your life and try to control everything in your life instead of flowing along with life. You like to do everything alone or have no trust or don't think they will be able to do the task as good as you. You can also be very judgemental of others and have no ability to empathise with others.

Physically to help balance walking in nature with no devices and let your mind quieten, meditation helps clear and repair the crown chakra, deep breathing exercise using your exhaling breath to exhale any anger you may have towards a situation or person, decluttering your living space can also help clear your mind. Learning to see the glass half full meaning to find the good in all situations – living your life with a grateful mind.

Foods to help your crown chakra are dried fruits, dates, nuts, purple cabbage, purple grapes, mushrooms, garlic, ginger, coconut.

Affirmations to say
I trust my intuition and listen to the wisdom the universe provides me.
I am deeply and unconditionally loved by the universe.
I have faith that I will be aligned with the universe to provide all that I need.

Crystals to help the crown chakra are celestite, amethyst, clear quartz, labradorite, diamonds, pearls, selenite, white opals, obsidian, sugarlite and moonstone.

The essential oils for your crown chakra are frankincense, cedar wood, myrrh, sandalwood, melissa, lemongrass, jasmine, and lavender.

The yoga poses are inversion poses.

BELOW IS A QR CODE TO A MEDITATION
TO HELP YOU CLEAR AND INCREASE YOUR
VIBRATION IN YOUR CROWN CHAKRA

49 Higher Self Chakra

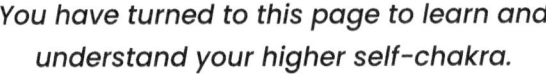

You have turned to this page to learn and understand your higher self-chakra.

The higher self-chakra is between 20–40cm above your crown chakra.

The higher self-chakra is our connection to our divine source, our soul self in heaven.

The higher self-chakra is our connection to the Archangel Angels, cross over loved ones, and the elemental kingdom.

The higher self-connection flows easier when we clear blocks from all our other chakras, meditate daily to clear our emotions that no longer serve us, this will make our vibrational energy higher to be able to connect into our higher self.

This chakra is different to all other chakras. Everyone has a higher self-chakra but not all souls on Earth will have a desire to connect to their higher self. Connecting to your higher self is a journey of self-discovery, it is clearing all your chakra blockages, facing all other negative emotions you have had in your life so far – clearing past family relations, past lover relationships, friendships that have failed, personality traits you don't like in yourself and personality traits you don't like in others. Allow love into your life and learning to love yourself unconditionally. Gratitude and being optimistic as a part of your thinking always and flowing with the flow of the universe. Having high integrity when dealing with others.

Meditation is a daily practice, however, concentrate on meditations that are clearing your chakra systems, meditations that will help you clear past hurts, meditations to help you connect to the Archangels angels, your higher self and spirit guide, meditations to help you connect to the elemental kingdom. Mindfulness meditations are great, but they will not help you connect to our higher self. When you connect with your higher self you will be able to hear your higher self-voice to help you guide you in your life.

Sitting in any ceremony where you take a drug or "plant medicine" to help you connect to your higher self is cheating and great karma is attached to this. In my experience as a healer this is the absolute worst way to connect to your higher self, and the quickest way to suffer from depression, as you will feel the great high from connecting to your higher self but after a few days, your energy will crash, making you feel the lowest of lows and vulnerable to dark energies attaching to you.

To connect to your higher self, you will have no addictions especially to alcohol, cigarettes, any forms of drugs, porn, or any other low vibrations lifestyle habit.

Physically to help balance, within your life meditation will be a daily practice. Eating well and great filtered water intake 2-3 litres daily. Walking or taking the time to be in nature to quieten the mind. Looking after your body to prevent any prescription drugs. Having a functional clean home.

Affirmations to say

I am dedicated to becoming the best version of myself with positive daily activities to help me connect to my higher self.

I'm here on Earth to achieve my highest vibrational soul energy.

I'm dedicated to daily practices to connect to my highest self. Universe, please help me clear all of my souls' lessons on Earth.

Crystals to help to help to connect to your higher self – pearls, amethyst, rose quartz, selenite, especially on your bedside table, aquamarine rose, citrine, diamonds, opals and clear quartz.

The essential oils to help to connect to your higher self are lavender, frankincense, sandalwood, myrrh.

The yoga poses corpse pose, rabbit pose, tree pose, and lotus pose.

BELOW IS A QR CODE TO A MEDITATION TO HELP YOU CLEAR AND INCREASE YOUR VIBRATION IN YOUR HIGHER SELF-CHAKRA

50 Earth Star Chakra

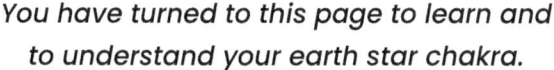

You have turned to this page to learn and to understand your earth star chakra.

The earth star chakra is located below your feet, one metre into Mother Earth and vibrates to the colour of platinum silver.

The earth star is important to physically connect to everyday as it connects you to the multi-dimensional spirit of Mother Earth or some call her Gaia and a connection to all other living beings here on Earth. When you connect to your earth star you have a close connection to the magic and mystery of Earth and to the elemental energy.

This chakra is essential when you are wanting to evolve spiritually and wanting to connect with you higher self. As you meditate more, your energy vibrates higher, and you will need to ground yourself to help stay in your physical body. E.g., when you see an evolved person, but they seem off with the pixies, it could be they are out of body and need to ground their energies into their earth star chakra.

Physically grounding into Mother Earth will help you if you're a little clumsy or lose your balance. If you have a terrible sense of direction or if you find you lose your train of thought or get your words jumbled or cannot think clearly. Go on the grass and reconnect into your earth star with the exercise I've given below. This is also great to use if your travelled on a plane to another country and feel out of body. Also, good if you have had a car accident or any physically accident and feel beside yourself.

HOW TO CONNECT TO YOUR EARTH STAR

Ask God or the divine creator for a column of white light all the way through you, all the way down to your earth star. Then ask rich platinum energy to come back up through your feet into your body and back up to the divine creator or God. You will have been connected to your mother earth star and the divine creator. Take some deep breaths in through your nose and out through your nose, feeling the connection you have.

Swimming in the ocean or river, walking on the beach or in nature will help you reconnect with your earth star. If you're not near but you have access to a bath, having a bath with Empson salts can also ground your energy into your earth star.

BELOW IS A QR CODE TO A MEDITATION TO HELP YOU CLEAR AND INCREASE YOUR VIBRATION IN YOUR EARTH STAR CHAKRA

PART SEVEN

Activating Your Intuition and Clairs

51 Clairvoyant

You have turned to this page to understand what clairvoyant is.

Clairvoyant is a French word meaning 'clear seeing'. This means you can see visions in your third eye. You can be gifted with being clairvoyant from a young age and can see visions in your third eye or you have great daydreams. Most can meditate to train and activate your third eye and clairvoyant vision and abilities.

Some signs that you have abilities:

- You had an imaginary friend a child.
- You can visualise your tasks, goals and dreams and bring them into reality by your manifesting skills.
- You can see people's auras.
- You appreciate beautiful places and things.
- You have lucid dreams and feel like your astral travel or project.
- You can visualise and daydream easily.
- You can meditate and easily see visions and colours.
- If you try to help someone, you can get a vision in your mind/third eye on how to help them or give suggestions.
- You get a feeling that something's not right when you are looking at something, something looks off, so you decide not to go to the place or event.

TO HELP ACTIVATE YOUR THIRD EYE AND YOUR CLAIRVOYANT ABILITIES

Meditating daily and connecting to your spirit guide and higher self. The spirit guide and the third eye meditations to help activate your clairvoyance. It also will help open your clairvoyant when you get a vision to take it seriously and take note of what you see and see if it happens.

I was blessed to be born with my vision but to be able to do this as a job/career. I had to meditate daily for years and to start to trust and journal my visions. Around friends I felt comfortable and trusted I started to say what I saw. This built my faith in my abilities. Now every day I meditate for my client and with my higher self and guides in the heavens, to show me what they want me to talk to about the client.

Crystals to help your clairvoyance Amethyst, labradorite, aquamarine, opals, fluorite, moonstone, sugitite, celestite.

Affirmations

Everyday I'm becoming more clairvoyant.
I trust my visions I see to help guide my life.

BELOW IS A QR CODE TO A MEDITATION TO HELP YOU ACTIVATE ALL OF YOU CLAIRS

52 Clairsentience

*You have turned to this page to
understand what clairsentience is.*

Clairsentience is the ability to receive an intuitive feeling, or you may sense it before someone feels it. E.g., you may pass someone and get either a good feeling or a bad feeling about them. Clairsentience is all about how you feel in a situation. You may also have this happen when you hug or touch someone. It also may activate when you go to a place and either love the energy of the place or feel the energy does not feel right or your do not feel comfortable. These feelings are a knowing you have. You may be conscious of these feelings, or unconsciously aware that you have this ability. You may even call this your gut instinct, but it feels stronger, and you have more confidence with what you are feeling.

    A tip for clairsentience is to stay away from negative humans or environments, as it can bring your good vibrations down and infiltrate your own state. You may start to act or feel like them. It is very important for you to be very conscious of where you go when you are clairsentient. E.g., going to a funeral, can make you feel exhausted for days. Being around everyone's sadness can really affect your energy vibration and your chakra system. Going to a place where alcohol is served or where people may be on recreational drugs, can make you feel unsettled or make your energy vibration feel low. Last example is going to a large concert with thousands of people attending, this can make you feel overwhelmed at the concert or after the concert; or you may feel so tired you just want to sleep.

    A way to increase your clairsentience, is to feel the places you are in and take time to acknowledge and understand how you feel.

To gauge how you feel around people in your life. It is best not to feel into other people's energy when you are out shopping, but if you are around friends and family and you sense something is wrong with them you could lean into what you are feeling about them. If you feel comfortable, ask them about it to see if your senses are correct about what you are feeling from them. This will help increase your ability of being clairsentient and validate that this gift is increasing within you.

BELOW IS A QR CODE TO A MEDITATION TO HELP YOU ACTIVATE ALL OF YOU CLAIRS

53 Clairaudience

You have turned to this page to help you understand what clairaudience is and how to awaken your ability to be clairaudient.

Clairaudience is the ability to perceive by hearing, your inner hearing. Clairaudience also means that you can communicate with spirits and angels. This will also increase greatly when you connect to your higher self and can communicate with them. This helps greatly if you are wanting to become a spiritual medium, clairvoyant, or psychic.

Some other ways to know you have clairaudience abilities are:

- Sensitive to noise.
- Hear bells, talking or ring at random times, when no one is around.
- Hear sounds that are inaudible to others.
- Naturally drawn to music.
- You sometimes can hear a noise or sound that triggers you to a past life.

I've had times when I've possibly dreamt a conversation prior to having it. Or in a meditation my higher self and guides have shown me a conversation – what to say to a certain person when I see them as a client. I've had times when I just heard the word no, so I've changed my mind to what I was about to do. All these times something has happened and I'm glad I listened to my Clairaudience.

WAYS TO HELP YOU BECOME MORE CLAIRAUDIENT

Meditation will help you get to converse with your higher self and spirit guides. It is time to quieten the mind to hear your clairaudience. Doing laps in a pool, focusing on the black line, and letting your inner voice channel through. Walking in nature or going for a walk to quieten the mind. I personally love snow skiing, for me is so quiet and peaceful.

It is taking the time to have quite time, to let the messages flow in. It saddens me to see most humans always connected to their electronic devices.

This can start with a word or a phase that keeps popping into your mind, or you start to sing a song in your head. It may be for you to listen and see what the words mean to you. The song could be to remember a good time in your life and to bring the positive energy from that time, or it could be to revisit a time in your life where you need to let go of negative emotions or feelings, to lift your vibration.

BELOW IS A QR CODE TO A MEDITATION TO HELP YOU ACTIVATE ALL OF YOU CLAIRS

54 Claircognition

You have turned to this page to understand and to help you develop your claircognition.

This is the ability for a person to acquire psychic knowledge without knowing how or why they know it.

Signs that you are claircognition

- You have great gut instincts and are always or most of the time correct.
- You can predict events on gut instinct/feelings or e.g., how the evening will end up.
- You just feel that whatever decision you are making for your life will be great.
- You can tell humans are lying or you can tell when a person is a good or bad person.
- You have ideas or solutions come to you, but you have no idea or understanding about this topic.
- You often already know before your friend or family member speaks, what they are going to say and what topic they are going to talk about.
- You will see a situation and know what or how it will end.
- You often like to sleep on a problem, and you will often then wake up with a solution.

WAYS TO HELP IMPROVE YOUR ABILITIES OF BEING CLAIRCOGNIZANT

Meditate with your spirit guides and higher self and ask them for solutions to your problems.

Ask your spirit guide and higher self for guides for a situation in your life and see if it is then shown to you. When you start to get a 'knowing' journal, you can then start build confidence with what you felt to be true; or know what you hear from your higher self or spirit guides will happen in the future.

Have quite moments in nature or whatever you love doing but allow for your inner knowing to have the right time to come through. No electronic devices in your ears will greatly help.

If you have children and they just know something will happen, please go with this, and allow their abilities to develop. I've always gone on the claircognitive abilities or the knowing they have. Let your knowing and instinct into your life freely, to allow you to have the most amazing life.

BELOW IS A QR CODE TO A MEDITATION TO HELP YOU ACTIVATE ALL OF YOU CLAIRS

55 Intuition and Gut Instinct

You have turned to this page to understand intuition and gut instinct but also for you to start to use your own intuition/gut instinct.

The meaning of intuition is the ability to understand something instinctively, without the need for conscious reasoning. I believe a large part of our soul coming to Earth is to learn how to listen and feel and have faith in our own intuition.

It is hard if you grew up in a home, where you had no voice and were told what to do. Your instinct was not developed as a child. Or you have had a relationship with a person who constantly told you what to do or belittled you on your thoughts and feelings.

Start to listen to your gut feelings when you are making decisions. The only way to help develop it is to start to use it. Meditate to help purge out and emotions and feelings you have about a parent or relationship that destroy your confidence in your decision making or your ability to make decisions for yourself. Write a purge letter to help let go of any negative emotions of yourself will also help.

Successful people, for example, will say they always go on their intuition as to whether to buy an investment property or business. If you are a parent, you could have turned to this page to start to help your children start to use their intuition/gut instinct. If they don't want to hug someone because it doesn't feel right, go with it. So far in my parental experience, every time my children have said that it didn't feel right in their tummy and did not want to go (to an event or occasion), we later found out that something went wrong, and it turned out for the best for my children.

You can help to develop your intuition by taking the time to check in with your gut/solar plexus chakra. Really explore how whatever you are thinking about makes you feel.

Meditating daily to clear away any negative vibrational energy and any other blocks you may have in your solar plexus or clear any blocks from overpowering parents and working on your inner children or purging emotions away from relationships with your life partners. Meditating to ask yourself about decisions that are needed in your life and see what feels right for you.

Daily, start to check in with how you feel about what is happening in your life. If you have trouble saying no to people in your life, this can be hindering you gut instincts. Start by saying 'let me have a think about that', if you feel you don't want to do or help a certain person. Then call or text them later. You have a limited time on Earth and it is not all to help others. Some time is for you to enjoy your life and wonderful experiences here on Earth.

BELOW IS A QR CODE TO A MEDITATION TO HELP YOU ACTIVATE ALL OF YOU CLAIRS

PART EIGHT

Inner Children

56 Inner Child 0–7

You have turned to this page to start to explore and heal your Inner Child 0–7.

This inner child is in your base chakra, your red child.

As an adult, this is your flight/fight response. Is your flight or fight response high? This can be because you have had feelings (maybe you cannot remember) of being abandoned between the ages of 0–7. This could be from controlled crying as a baby or that both your parents had to go back to work and placed you in day-care from just months old. In my healing room, often I can still feel the abandonment energy from a person in their 40's from the way they were parented, especially if they felt abandoned.

If you suffer from any form of depression or lack of confidence, I want you to do the meditation below to see what feelings, memories and emotions come through in the meditation. If you find it hard to settle in one place as an adult. In your first seven years of life, did your family move around a lot or you slept at different family members' homes often? If you feel that you did not thrive between the ages of 0–7, I want you now to think about what you felt was missing from your family. Take time this week to do something you felt was missing in your childhood. It could be colouring in with a parent, playing outside with a parent, painting and getting messy with craft. Now as an adult you don't have to do this with your parent, but please try to do something you felt was missing from your childhood. It is like you are reparenting your inner child.

Are you motivated to work hard to buy things in your life to impress others? This is also from your childhood. Especially if, between the ages 0–7, you grew up in a home with not a lot of money or your felt lack in your childhood. Try to identify within yourself why you are buying certain things or wanting to live a certain lifestyle. What is your motivation?

If you do not have time to do the meditation below on the QR code, please do this little exercise now.

Ask God or the divine creator for a column of white light, then in your mind's eye, visualise beautiful healing red energy from God or the divine creator to heal your base chakra, your red inner child. If anything comes to mind that was negative about your childhood, breath out the negative energy into the red columns of energy.

BELOW IS A QR CODE TO A MEDITATION TO HELP HEAL YOUR INNER CHILD 0–7

57 Inner child 7–14

You have turned to this page to start to explore and heal your inner child 7–14.

This inner child is in your sacral chakra, your orange child.

As an adult, do you have any issues with commination or miscommunication? This is a skill developed between the ages of 7–14. Now as an adult, if you have trouble with communication, it is more than likely because the skill was not learnt between the ages of 7–14. Especially if your parents did not listen to you or engage in conversations with you. Your temper associated with communication is also developed at this age, if you are an angry communicator and don't think before you speak, explore what happened when you were younger. Did your parents yell at you a lot? Or you were not allowed to share your feelings? Now, as an adult, do you over share?

Lack of self-confidence can also be from the inner child 7–14, especially if you suffer from moments of jealousy, comparing yourself to others or wonder why they are doing so well for themselves, and you are not. Poverty mindset or the feelings of being poor are developed between the age of 7–14. You would have understood your social status in the world, and it is possible your parents would have often said 'we can't afford it'. This would have been engrained into your thinking about how you see yourself in the world. This can make you become very materialistic and work hard to have what you didn't have as a child or overcompensate with your children and give them everything you didn't have.

You can also accept the poverty mindset and may simply accept what the government hands to you and just make do with what you have. We all have the same opportunities in life, if you are not happy with what you have, start to work through all your money blocks and limiting thoughts you have. If you want to re-educate yourself, start to look at the course or careers that interest you.

My best advice is to stay in your own lane and focus on your own life and ways to help improve your thinking process and becoming the person you want to be. You do not have to accept the life your parents gave you or compromise what you want out of life.

Money habits form and the emotions you have to money. Overspending to feel better can be associated with how and when your parents gave you gifts or helped you through disappointments in your life.

Working on your inner child can be confronting, here are some tips to help you.

Write a purge letter to your parents. Let out all your feelings and emotions of frustration or hurts to help your inner child heal. Once you've written the letter, then burn it. As the letter burns, let all your emotions go into the fire as well. Handwriting the letter is better than typing on the computer. You may write 3-4 letters of purge from your childhood. Write as many purge letters as you need.

You can also do visualisations with you as the parent of your inner child and re parent yourself. The way you communicate, your relationship with money, giving your inner child confidence.

Read many self-help books to help you become the very best version of yourself.

**BELOW IS A QR CODE TO A MEDITATION
TO HELP HEAL YOUR INNER CHILD 7–14**

58 Inner Child 14-21

You have turned to this page to start to explore and heal your inner child 14-21.

This is your solar plexus child, your yellow child.

Boundaries are set in the solar plexus; do you have good boundaries? Are you too easy going or too rigid with your boundaries? Do you need to write a list of your boundaries for friends, family, and relationships? Does your confidence waver, in a situation or around certain people in your life? Did your parent build you up to have great confidence and self-esteem?

If your parents made you feel not good enough or belittled, you and made you feel any lacking thoughts about yourself and now as an adult you suffer from low self-esteem or low confidence in your ability, please start to do some purge letters to your parents about how they made your feel and then burn the letters. If you feel you need to see a therapist to help, that is ok as well. I would suggest starting to focus on your self-talk, start to talk to yourself like you are talking to your best friend. If you do say something negative to yourself, say cancel that thought. This will help to build your confidence within yourself.

Did any addictions or unhealthy habits start between the ages of 14-21? The solar plexus is the chakra in our body where we hold our personal power. We form these habits between the ages of 14-21 to cope with our life, especially our home life. Eating disorders often occur when you have parents who you felt were over controlling or told you how unattractive you were. Alcoholism or drug taking happens to numb yourself or because of the self-hatred.

If as an adult you still have these abusive habits, please explore where you think it started and how you think you can help heal and become healthier.

Do you make great decisions in your life, or have you chosen consistently the wrong type of partner, the wrong job or have financially made bad choices?

If you have chosen wrong life partners, I want you to write an intentions list of what you want in a partner.

If you have bad habits around finances, seek a friend to help you or a financial advisor to help you get your finances in order. Read some books around money management. Not many parents teach their children about money management or how to budget. My simplest tip is having a tally in your phone, your expenses have to be less than your income you are earning.

Anxiety can also be start in your solar plexus between the ages 14-21, if you do suffer from anxiety, see if there's a moment you can remember when it started.

Some other ways to help release low vibration energy from you from the ages of 14-21 is you can throw rocks into the ocean, beach, river, or lake, as you are throwing the rocks in yell out all your frustrations, feelings and emotions that no longer serve you. Or write words or sentences that no longer serve you and throw the words into a bin, even better if you had a little fireplace or outside fire pit to throw away all the feelings and emotions that no longer serve you.

BELOW IS A QR CODE TO A MEDITATION
TO HELP CLEAR THE NEGATIVE ENERGY
FOR YOUR INNER CHILD 14–21

If you find this meditation hard, listen to the meditation while walking. Walk in a place where you don't stop and chat to people so you can hold your focus on the meditation.

PART NINE

Healing

59 House Clearing

You have turned to this page to start to clear the energy of your home, car or place of work.

Negative energy can make your home feel stagnant or a place you don't like being in. House clearings are so important to start to include in your weekly cleaning your home especially if you have had an argument, a relationship break up, you've had other people stay in your home, you have just moved into your home, or your home feels dense in energy.

Here are some steps to clear your home (best to do this when no one's home or ask them to go outside while you are clearing the home):

1. Ask Archangel Michael to place a golden net over your home.
2. Start in the lounge room. Ask God or the Divine creator for a column of white light around you, then ask Archangel Michael to step into your white column and feel it expand.
3. Now just in the lounge room ask Archangel Michael to clear all the negative energy in the lounge room and clear any lost souls or negative entities. Archangel Michael is clearing this for you now. You may just stand in the middle of the lounge room, or you may walk around the room while Archangel Michael in clearing for e.g. walking up and down the room slowly.
4. Once you have completed this do, exactly the same process in the kitchen, hallways, bedrooms, bathrooms toilets, open the linen cupboards and pantry to clear away the negative energy. Also include the garage if it's under the same roof as the house.

5. Once you have done all the rooms, walk into each room to feel the energy and see if it feels good, if not you can redo the process with Archangel Michael.
6. Thank Archangel Michael for his help today.
7. You can then smudge the house with a sage stick or sage leaves, going into each room of the house.
8. Stand at each doorway of your home, include door and sliding doors and you can ask Lady Portia to place beautiful energy at each doorway to attract love, joy and abundance into your home. This will also stop negative energy entering your home as well.
9. Open all the windows, to let in abundance.
10. Burn some of your essential oils.
11. If a room still feels heavy with energy, you can place a bowl with a cup of salt to draw the negative energy into the salt water, leave 2 days and then tip the salt water down the drain.

60 Living with Gratitude

*You have turned to this page to
focus on living with gratitude.*

Living with grateful hear can change the vibration of your soul and the life you have on Earth. We have all had low, horrible moments in our lives. The best way to help move forward is to focus in the good and focus on what you already have. When you start to do this, you will focus on the gratitude you have in your life, this will then become a habit that you will only see the good in a situation. All my day, I live in gratitude, I am thankful I live in a country with flushing toilets and water that I can drink from the tap. I am grateful I have food to eat and clothes to wear, that I have a choice of clothing and shoes to wear.

Do you look to the positive in a situation or do you look for all the negatives in a situation? Life can be so much easier if you look for the positive and what you are grateful for in the situation.

If you have had moments in your life when you felt depressed or just feeling low, I bet you had extraordinarily little thoughts of gratitude or to look for the positive.

The most success and the happiest people are the people who only focus on the positive and have a grateful heart.

Teach this to your children, friends and family, the more people who live in gratitude, the better the vibration on the planet will be. Ask them often, 'what are you grateful for today.'

Tell your friends, family, co-workers, shop assistance how grateful you are for their love, friendship, there great service that they are providing you. People stay where they are loved and felt needed.

Being in gratitude in your life, gives your resilience when times become tough in your life, this is also called the attitude of gratitude. Looking for the positive in all situations make life like living you are living on holidays.

BELOW IS A QR CODE TO A MEDITATION TO HELP YOU RECOGNISE THE GRATITUDE IN YOUR LIFE

61 Past life Clearing

*You have turned to this page to help
clear and heal your past lives to help you
have a peaceful life, on this journey.*

Do you have moments when you have déjà vu or feel like you have done this before? You could also experience moments in your life when you have extreme fear or worry about something, but you have no reason you have this fear.

In relationships, you can have a huge attraction and connection with someone, the relationship from the start is intense and then the relationship can turn toxic. In a past life your relationship did not work out and you're both recontracted in the heavens to try again, the meeting again can be intense, but you still have the same issues to work out. This can be for all types of relationships with siblings, friends, parents, lovers, co-workers. Some people you meet, you will instantly dislike them for no reason, why. They could possibly be from a past life. I find this topic so fascinating. Have a think in your life, is there someone in it who you had a huge attraction too or instantly did not like?

Sometimes when a relationship ends, your heart and soul just cannot get over the heart break. Your head can understand the logic of why you were not compatible, but you can't get over the heart break. This can be because you both had a contract in this life to try to work out your differences. This can be a huge sadness in your heart chakra, but you alone cannot make the relationship work. To help clear the energy for the rest of your life you can do the meditation below o help clear out the heart break from your heart chakra or write or journal your heart break and really let go, knowing that you can re try in another lifetime.

Steps to help clear the heart break or any relationships that is a struggle:

1. Ask God or the divine creator for a column of white light all the way through you, all the way down to Mother Earth.
2. Ask Archangel Michael to step into the column of you are standing in. When you feel his presence then ask Archangel Michael to clear away all the cords, negative energy, and heart-break from all the people you have had issues with. Taking some deep breaths and allow Archangel Michael to clear your energy from your chakras.
3. Now ask Archangel Raphael to step into the column and help heal all your heart hurts, clear away the pain for this lifetime and to help your heart heal and to easily accept what has happened. Take some deep breaths and breath in Archangel Raphael's healing energy.
4. Thank Archangel Michael and Archangel Raphael for the help today.

You can do this process as many times as you like.

BELOW IS A QR CODE TO THE PAST LIFE CLEARING MEDITATION

62 Vagus Nerve

You have turned to this page to focus energy on your vagus nerve.

If this nerve is out of alignment on an energetic level, you can feel on edge or life can feel overwhelming. Let me explain on an energetic level about the vagus nerve. It runs through most of your organs within your body. It starts at the base of your spine and the last nerve is at your anus. When you have had a fright e.g., a car accident or any physical injury or you experience any type of trauma or loss you can really upset your vagus nerve on a spiritual level. You can experience a heavy weight on your chest area, or you have moments of anxiousness. Clearing the vagus nerve is also extremely helpful if you suffer from anxiety, and nervous related issues within your body like irritable bowel syndrome, asthma, stomach issues.

Many years ago, Archangel Raphael showed me how to help people relax their vagus nerve. Many clients when they return to see me have expressed how much more relaxed and peaceful, they have felt. Archangel Raphael wanted me to show more people now more than ever, how to help themselves.

This is be done in a quiet, home environment, sitting or standing:

1. Ask God or the divine creator for a column of white light, all the way through you.
2. Ask Archangel Raphael to step into the column of white light you in.
3. Now ask Archangel Raphael to place his green healing energy all the way through you.

4. Take some deep breaths in, and breath in the beautiful green healing energy.
5. Now ask Archangel Raphael to place his healing green energy all the way through your vagus nerve.
6. Visualise the vagus nerve in your mind's eye and ask Archangel Raphael to send healing energy through your vagus nerve.
7. Feel the vagus nerve reset back to perfect balance.
8. Take some more deep breaths and feel the wave of healing energy wash over you.
9. Thank Archaeal Raphael for his time and healing today.

You can do this exercise as many times as you like.

BELOW IS A QR CODE TO A MEDITATION TO HELP HEAL YOUR VAGUS NERVE SYSTEM

63 Vibrating High

You have turned to this page as the guides and Archangels are noticing and feeling all the hard work you've done to raise your vibration.

The higher your vibration, the easier it is to communicate with your spirit guides, higher self, dragons, unicorns, the Archangels and the Ascended Masters. The quickest way to raise your vibration is to mediate daily and stay in your integrity and truth.

Vibrating high also helps you to manifest much more easily. If you have not already, please write a goals list or create a vision board and look at these daily. Focus on the possibility of all that you can achieve and begin to create anything you want. When your vibration is high, you may be asked by your higher self or one of the Archangels to assist a help group or charity. At this time, you may also start to think about starting a meditation group or look for a spiritual development coach or a clairvoyant course. You may feel a pull to learn how to heal others and possibly look at spiritual development as a career.

Be sure to continue to mediate daily and talk with your spiritual team all day, every day. When you get messages from your spirit guides and higher self, write them down. When they come true, this gives you validation that your intuition and connection is strengthening.

Be proud of yourself. Your hard work and dedication to improving yourself is starting to show.

64 Medicine Healing

Listen to your body's needs, become your own medicine healer within.

You are your own medicine healer and the best advocate for your body. Life gets so busy, with daily demands, we forget to listen to what our body needs. What is your own intuition feeling about what we are needing in your life to feel good within your body? It's time to start to feel and go within, to feel what we are needing for your body, mind and spirit.

Do you feel you have balance between your work, family and your own time. Are you taking time to nurture yourself? Do you agree to help others and then get cranky with yourself on the way to help them. Are you a people pleaser?

Make a mental note or write a list of all the ways you can help you feel happy and physically relaxed. Write at least 12 items – 1 per month on a list to nurture you per year or 52 items on your list – one per week. It can be as easy as have 1 hour per week to lay or sit with your feet on the grass or sand to relax on feel one with nature.

Are you eating and drinking filter water to fuel your body with great nutrients? Do you need to start to slowly eliminate alcohol, soft drinks, energy drinks or recreational drugs from your life? Are you around toxic people? Do you need to start to change or lesson time with some of your group of friends or family. Remember to share your time with people who lift you up or make you feel good about yourself. We only get one body in this life, it's time to be more conscious of what you are needing to live pain-free and with vitality. Take the time to write a list of all the changes you are needing in your life to have the best life experience in your healthy body.

65 Ancestry Healing

Clearing family from curses, trauma, shame, regrets, addictions and abuse.

Do you see a pattern within your family tree? Is it shame or the masculine or feminine being suppressed. Did your parents or grandparents have difficulty with money or a poverty mindset? Has there been many generations of divorce or cheating partners or poor choices in life partners? Has your family linage had problems with addictions – alcohol, drugs, gambling? Is there a family member always trying to cause disharmony with the family? Has there been sexual or domestic violence within your family? Has your lineage been in the fight or flight mode due to experiencing war or violence in their country?

It's time to heal all the negative ancestry energy for you and your future generations. Take deep breaths and ask the divine creator to a column of white light all around you.

Ask Archangel Michael, to help clear away from yourself, your family and past generations on both side any dark negative energy that's not for your family's highest good.

Feel Archangel Michael clearing away all the negative energy, cords and attachment's now. With your breath, feel this releasing.

Taking some more deep breaths and call in Archangel Rapheal, to help heal all the trauma from your family, placing his healing through you and your linage to heal any forms of abuse, addiction, shame, regret and negative emotions. Image he is placing a green bubble of healing energy through you and past generations.

Asking now Archangel Metatron to bless your family with good fortune, good health and to be abundant on all levels of life, for yourself and future generations.

Thank the Archangels for assisting you today.

You can do this as many times as you like to help heal past generational hurts and negative emotions.

66 Limbic Healing

Archangel Mariel healing our nervous system.

The limbic system is in the centre of our brain closer to the eyes. Spiritually this holds and stores our emotions, traumas and what we think we deserve it life.

It's time to heal your spiritual limbic system to help release any stored emotions that no longer serve you. These emotions can be anxiety, childhood memories, trauma, abuse and any other negative emotion that you are feeling.

Ask Archangel Mariel to help place her magenta pink and gold energy over and through your limbic system to help heal these stored negative emotions from your limbic system. Take deep breaths and ask Archangel Mariel to place her golden and magenta pink energy over your head to help remove all the trauma from your limbic system now. Give to Archangel Mariel your thoughts and feeling that you are ready to let go off and for you also ask Archangel Mariel to remove and other stored emotions that no longer serve you.

The heavens want the best for you and so does your higher self. Please take small steps daily to help let go off any negative emotions that effects your nervous system.

Archangel Mariel also want to you focus on your self-talk – how you talk to yourself is another way to help heal your limbic system. When you catch yourself talking poorly to yourself, tell yourself to cancel that thought. Start to talk to yourself like you are talking to your best friend.

You can ask daily Archangel Mariel to place her golden and purple energy around your limbic to help clear trauma, old patterning and your belief systems.

67 Timeline Healing

Archangel Rapheal healing.

With the help of Archangel Rapheal, you are now being asked to help heal times in your life that caused you sadness, hurt, trauma and any other types of hurt or emotional distress you may have felt in your life.

Image your life is like a mathematics ruler. Number 1 to however old you are now. In your mind's eye, feel or see in your mind's eye what numbers along the ruler that need help and healing. It might be consciously that you know, or your sub conscious may be showing your numbers that need healing that you have repressed. The numbers you are being shown are the age of you that needs healing.

Ask Archangel Raphael to place healing energy over that age in your past. If you can remember that time in your life, visualise yourself and image Archangel Raphael's green energy over you at that age. Let go of any emotions you are feeling from that time to Archangel Rapheal. With your breath, you can breathe the emotions out of your physical body. Letting go of emotions that have been stored within your time line, will help you feel emotionally lighter and help your soul grow and heal from any negative situation or emotions you have stored within your body.

PART TEN

Archangels

68 Archangel Ariel

Colour Vibration: pink and soft blue.

Helps the heart chakra and the animal kingdom.

Element – water.

Crystals to help Archangel Ariel rose quartz, rhodochrosite, pink opal, peach moonstone.

Archangel Ariel is often called the Lioness of God. She loves helping humans, animals, and environmental causes, she is also called the angel of nature. You can always call on Archangel Ariel if you are worried about your situation regarding your personal needs such as shelter, money, and your supplies to survive. You can also ask Archangel Ariel to help when a natural disaster has happened, and humans and animals need help. You could ask Archangel Ariel to help provide people with the correct divisions and for enough people to be sent to help with the natural disaster.

Archangel Ariel comes into my healing room to help people who have forgotten why they have come to Earth. They have forgotten their souls' goals and lessons, they wanted to learn here on Earth. She ignites the reason my clients have come to Earth and to help people reach their full potential.

Archangel Ariel also reawakens people's souls to see the absolute beauty in nature, here on Earth to see and notice all the beauty in the birds, wildlife, animals, plants, and flowers, that we can often take for granted.

If you are worried about a place on Earth that you feel is being destroyed, pray to Archangel Ariel to help, place the right authorities to stop this happening.

Archangel Ariels can also help you develop your clairvoyant and psychic abilities, you can ask her to help you while you are meditating, or I find it easily to connect to Archangel Ariel when I am walk in nature or at the beach. You can also ask her to help open your clairvoyant eye if you are a practitioner before you start seeing your clients for the day.

Archangel Ariel can also give you strength when you have had disappointment with a friendship that been destroyed or a heartbreak over a breakup or a loss of job or a business that did not work or make enough profit for you to continue with it. You can ask her to give you strength to move forward. She can bestow onto you, courage and confidence to move forward in your life.

You can wear the above crystals in your pocket to help Archangel Ariel bring in her healing energy into your body.

69 Archangel Mary

Colour Vibration: aquamarine.

Helps the heart chakra.

Crystals to help aquamarine, rose quartz, jade, emeralds.

Archangel Mary and Mother Mary I believe are the same angel or Archangel. Archangel Mary or Mother Mary, when they come into my healing room are surrounded by so much aquamarine energy, light, and unicorns.

If you have difficult relationships with females and especially your mother or your mother has passed and gone to the heavens, Mary energy can help your heart feel the love of a mother. You can simply ask the Mary energy for her aquamarine cloak of love, protection, and support anytime you feel you need it. If you see a child or family who need extra love, protection and support you can ask the for the Divine Feminine Healing of the Marys to be sent to help them with what they need or ask for an aquamarine cloak around the child or family. If you or if you are a practitioner and are helping a child with special needs or an ill child, ask the Marys for her aquamarine cloak of healing and her help for the child to be connected to the right teacher or support person they need to help have the best life here on Earth.

Many people have noted through time that they can smell roses when the Marys are around them, I can also say this happened for me when I am in my healing room and a client needs help from the Marys or when I am meditating, and they are giving me their healing energy. Anytime you need the strength of the divine feminine energy or a love like a mother's love, you can ask this of the Marys. If you have had difficult relationships with your mother, sisters or communicating with female energy ask for their help, support, and healing. Many times, I have asked for this help to give me support, love, encouragement to move forward in tough times, associated with other females and help with healing the relationship with my mother.

The Marys also love to bring balance or bring in the divine feminine energy into places that are unbalanced and have too much masculine energy. Please ask the Marys to bring in aquamarine energy into and say the name of the place, to help balance the energy in that area/place.

If you are a leader, ask the Marys to always help you lead with love and compassion in your heart and to give you the divine feminine leader energy – to lead with love and fairness.

BELOW IS A QR CODE TO A MEDITATION TO HELP YOU CONNECT WITH THE DIVINE FEMININE HEALING OF THE MARYS

70 Jesus – Christ Light

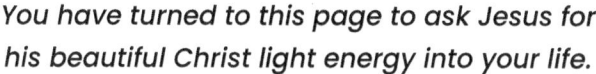

You have turned to this page to ask Jesus for his beautiful Christ light energy into your life.

Jesus is one of the ascended masters in the heavens who loves to share or offer his Christ light over people on Earth. Ask Jesus for his beautiful Christ light energy any time you need strength, courage to if you are in a situation now that need extra energy to help you create the life you want. You can also ask Jesus for his golden Christ light to be sent to someone you thinks needs his help.

If you feel worried, fearful or you are not feeling well or have been diagnosed with an illness or disease in your body, ask Jesus for his golden healing cloak of Christ light to help you have the best outcome for yourself.

You can also ask Jesus while you are meditating to help you lift your vibrations energy to help you with your spiritual healing abilities and to help you raise your vibrations to 5th dimensional energy.

If a world event or disaster happen that has people holding onto fear and worry, ask Jesus to send his Christ light energy to the place of disaster or visualise the planet Earth in your mind's eye surrounded or in golden bubble of Jesus Christ light energy.

The love and support I have received from Jesus and his healing Christ light has changed the direction of my life to lead me to my best life, I could not have even imaged this without the strength of connecting with Jesus and his Christ light. Please start to ask him into your life daily and see the difference in your life. His strength and support have given so many of my client's strength to lead their best life.

A sign that he is around you is if you see the number 33.

BELOW IS A QR CODE TO A MEDITATION TO HELP YOU CONNECT WITH JESUS – CHRIST LIGHT

71 Archangel Gabriel

Colour Vibration: red, orange, and yellow.

Helps the base, sacral and solar plexus chakra.

Element is water.

Crystals to help Archangel Gabriel is Citrine.

Archangel Gabriel is the Archangel to call upon when you have doubts about your spiritual abilities. In a meditation you can ask Archangel Gabriel to help clear and give you confidence that you are here on Earth to help others through your clairvoyant or physic abilities.

Archangel Gabriel also will help clear and unblock any negative energy, trauma or blockages in your base, sacral and solar plexus chakra, you can ask him to clear these chakras in your next meditation.

Archangel Gabriel can help you give you confidence and courage to follow your dreams and goals with your career. He has helped people in my healing room, with his blessing and energy to help then move forward with confidence to follow their dreams and souls' journey here on Earth. He is also known to help people upskill or re-educate them to follow their path of empowerment.

He also sends his beautiful energy to people who have had terrible parenting or have extremely low self-esteem, low self-worth, or no confidence. He places his golden energy over people to give the energy to move forward with confidence and an inner strength within them. Archangel Gabriel also loves helping you with inner child healing.

Archangel Gabriel also loves helping or holding energy for you if you are teaching or holding any form of spiritual teaching class or meditation class. He sparkles his energy around the room to help give confidence to students and to you to see your spiritual abilities.

72 Archangel Metatron

Colour Vibration: white, pink, and green swirls within the golden energy.

Helps the soul star chakra, stellar gateway.

Element – universal.

Crystals: Lapis Lazuli, Kyanite, Ladradorite.

Archangel Metatron is with you and wanting you to ask him for help and to acknowledge that he is here for you. Since 2012, Archangel Metatron presence has been felt here on Earth. He and Jesus are the two ascended masters who have been leading the way to help Earth become 5th dimensional energy. He and Jesus are seated next to God or the divine creator in the heavens. Archangel Metatron's special healing is called 'the white ray of light'. Please ask Archangel Metatron for his white ray of light when you are wanting to have a better connection with your spirit guide, higher self, dragon, and unicorn. He can also help you strengthen your clairvoyancy, psychic abilities, and the connection you have to the archangels.

When you have asked Archangel Metatron for help and have a better connection to your spiritual team and Archangels, your light vibration here on Earth will increase and help the planet increase to 5th dimensional energy. Archangel Metatron would also like to visit you while you are meditating. You can ask him for his white ray of light to help increase and clear your chakra system. Archangel Metatron oversees your soul star chakra; he can help you open your light body enlightenment – which means strengthen your bridge between Earth and the spiritual realms. Archangel Metatron can also help when children or people with special needs, require energy or to help their energy realign with the energy of Earth. You can ask Archangel Metatron to re-adjust the child's energy to have a better experience here on Earth. He also loves helping people who have mental health issues. You can ask Archangel Metatron to send his white ray of light to the person to help assist the person raise their vibration. If you feel, or a friend, family member or a client has felt like they have been overlaid with dark energy or they feel they are not in Gods light, Archangel Metatron can realign their soul back into pure white light.

BELOW IS A QR CODE TO A MEDITATION TO HELP YOU CONNECT WITH ARCHANGEL METATRON

73 Archangel Michael

Colour Vibration: royal blue.

Helps the throat chakra.

Element – fire sign.

Crystals to help Archangel Michael connect to you are sugilite and lapis.

Archangel Michael has many different roles here on Earth, his name who is like God. Archangel Michael will help you clear away all negative energy from your aura and body.

Here is a way you can ask Archangel Michael:

'Ask God or the divine creator for a column of white light all the way through you. Ask Archangel Michael to step into the column of white light you are visualising yourself in. Ask Archangel Michael to clear away any negative energy overlaid over you by other humans and to clear any lost souls or negative attachments from you. Take some deep breathes and allow Archangel Michael to do this for you.' Thank Archangel Michael and God for their help today.

Archangel Michael also loves to place a blue bubble or his blue cloak of protection around you every morning to keep your energies safe from others throughout your day. I suggest you make this a habit after you have done your morning bathroom actives and you are washing your hands. Anchor in this with a habit you do every day, so you keep your energies clear and protected every day. This is so important if you are wanting to increase your vibrational energy and grow more spiritually.

Archangel Michael also loves to help when you have fear and doubt about the decisions you are making in your life. You can ask Archangel Michael to help you make the right decisions for your life. He loves helping you clear your home or workspace of negative energy. Archangel Michael also loves helping you heal and clear negative energy from your throat chakra. Do you have conversations in your head about what you should have said to the person you have a conflict with or with whom you are angry? Archangel Michael is also the archangel to help if you have any physical problems with your throat and neck area, especially if you overshare and say too much to people or do not express your thoughts and feelings and suppress your feelings.

You can ask Archangel Michael to clear away all the negative energy from your throat chakra and then channel in his beautiful royal blue healing energy into your throat chakra.

Archangel Michael and Archangel Raphael are the two archangels that have helped me the most with all the clients I have seen over the years.

74 Archangel Nathaniel

Colour Vibration: red and orange.

Helps the heart chakra.

Element – fire.

Crystals to help Archangel Nathaniel energy to come into your presents – carnelian, orange, calcite, garnet, rutilated Quartz.

Archangels Nathaniel's name means Gift of God. He is also known as the angel of fire, the angel of energy, the angel of purification, the angel of divinity and the angel of life purpose. The heavenly councils Archangel Nathaniel works with are universal spiritual law of cause and effect, which is the karmic council. Archangel Nathaniel helps you if you are needing help if you are a procrastinator or not sure how to start a project or are needing confidence and motivation. Ask him to help you visualise what needs to be done, to complete your project.

'Archangel Nathaniel help me or guide me to easily find the motivation to start and finish the project.'

Archangel Nathaniel has come to Earth to help people find their purpose. To help people find their joy, happiness, love, passion with passion here on Earth. He is also an archangel who wants all of us to help each other. When we can, especially in a community crisis. E.g., a flood, bush fires, around the holiday season, he wants you to spread love, joy and help where you can. You can also help

Archangel Nathaniel by helping people realize their worth and to build other humans up. This is one of Archangel Nathaniel's mission here on Earth.

If you are a practitioner or help people with energy healings, Archangel Nathaniel can help you heal people when you use crystals on their chakra system. In my healing room, I ask Archangel Nathaniel to channel his healing energy into their heart chakra, especially if my client has lost hope and their soul light has been blown out. Archangel Nathaniel will help reignite their heart chakra to see hope, possibilities and to help increase the persons self-worth and self-esteem.

75 Archangel Raphael

Colour Vibration: emerald green.

Helps the heart chakra.

Element – air.

Crystals to help Archangel Raphael connect with you are malachite, citrine, adventurine and yellow calcite.

Archangel Raphael is the healing angel in the heaven. He is the archangel who helps heal my clients in my healing room. I'm blessed that Archangel Raphael helps with almost every client I see. He vibrates the energy of green and will place his beautiful healing energy into people's chakras to help increase peoples' love and peace and brings calmness over them. Archangel Raphael can also help someone who is heartbroken and has lost hope in their life. He will place his beautiful healing energy in their heart chakra, to bring hope and joy back into their life. Archangel Raphael is always happy to help you personally or if you are a practitioner and wanting to help others. He is an amazing archangel to help heal and repair chakra tears in people's chakra systems. Chakra tears can tear between each chakra, this can make you or your client have feeling of exhaustion, and they can have feelings of overwhelm or be overly emotional.

When asking Archangel Raphael for help, you can place your hands on or near each chakra on yourself or your client and ask Archangel Raphael to repair each chakra and repair and chakra tears within each chakra. If you or a client has an illness or disease in their body, you can pray with the client to ask Archangel Raphael to heal. In a prefect way take away (say the name of the illness or disease). If a loved one is sick, whether you are with them or they are far away, you can ask Archangel Raphael for his beautiful healing green energy to be placed around them, to help heal or offer pain relief, whatever your loved one is needing. If you are a practitioner or are opening a healing space that helps animals or humans, ask Archangel Raphael for his healing energy in and around the room or building.

76 Archangel Raziel

Colour Vibration: all the colours of the rainbow.

Helps the crown chakra.

Embodies – divine magic and esoteric understanding.

Crystals to help Archangel dark opal.

Archangel Raziel is known as the keeper of secrets and mysteries. His name means 'secret of God.' He is an ascended master who stands or is around God or the divine creator in the heavens, he is also a multi-dimensional archangel. Archangel Raziel is an extremely calm and patient archangel, one of Gods' helpers who helps souls crosser over to heaven and to help give comfort to the families who have lost loved ones.

He is the archangel you can pray or meditate to, to ask for help financially or to help unblock any financial or prosperity block within you or your family.

Archangel Raziel will help you to unblock your spiritual abilities and help you interpret your past lives and what is their meaning to help you in your current soul life. You can also ask for his help while meditating to help show your souls past lives.

In my healing room Archangel Raziel will often sprinkle his energy over my clients when they have a block in their creative flow or in this life meant to use their creative abilities. He never wants to be recognised or acknowledge by my clients, but if my clients thank me for their increases in finances or whatever Archangel Raziel did, I will always say it is my Archangel friends in the heavens. I never take credit for Archangel Raziel's magic and mystery he gives to my clients. He will not work with spiritual healers or clairvoyants who are in ego or do it for their own gain.

He is an amazing Archangel who, if you get the opportunity to feel his presence in a meditation, you should feel very blessed and incredibly grateful for his time spent with you.

77 Miriam Ascended Master

A Miriam healing is with you.

Miriam with our history is a portrait of courage, deep family connection, leadership and having faith in God or the divine creator. Miriam has been asked to be of help here on Earth. Miriam is a prophet and of the seven major female prophets in history, she is now with you to help you have the "Miriam effect".

She's witnessed the great miracles God performed through Moses and her guidance to help her save her brother's life. She's now coming back to Earth spiritually to help you have the Miriam effect on your life.

To bring Miriam into your energy vibration, take some breaths and ask Miriam to step into your energy field. With you, breathing deeply in and out she is bestowing on to you the courage to go in the direction your souls guided along. She is placing over you her energy for you to have the faith in yourself and to start to grow the love for yourself. Miriam is filling you up with faith love and courage, breath this in and feel it filling up your chakra system.

She's wanting you to have a life filled with love, faith and courage firstly for yourself and then to spread and teach this message to others. Miriam is now clearing within your energy fields any negative energy that you have about yourself or any situations and experiences you have had that wasn't for your highest good or that has affected your life path. Take some breaths and allow Miriam to take away this now, give those emotions to Miriam and allow her to replace those feeling with faith, love and courage. Miriam is now asking you if she can clear away with your breath, past generations wrongs, habits, abuse, and any other karma that has lowered the vibrational frequency within your family, take some breaths and allow Miriam to clear this away. Miriam and the divine creator are now bringing in unwavering faith that the universe will provide for you and your family.

Miriam can also remove reoccurring patterns that you can see in your family history. With your breath allow Miriam to place energy over you to help go through your DNA to help clear past generational patterns. Miriam is here to be of service to you any time you need faith in yourself and faith that the universe will provide for you.

It's time to be brave and courageous with Miriam helping you.

PART ELEVEN

The Alchemist Within

78 Sorcerer

It's time to be the sorcerer in your life.

You are the sorcerer in your life to create the most magical life. Today we call this manifesting.

Do you call on the archangels, the divine creator or God to help you achieve your goals, dreams and ambitions? Do you talk and feel positive about your dreams and goals?

To achieve your dreams and goals you must everyday think of what I have done today to achieve my dreams and goals. You can ask the below Archangels for help.

Ascended Master Lady Portia will help clear away negative karma and help send positive karma ahead of you to help keep your path in a golden energy and positive light.

Archangel Rapheal to help heal any areas of your life that needs healing that may stop you from achieving your dreams.

Keep asking the Archangels above to help clear away any negative emotional and negative feelings to unblock the energy that may be holding you back to achieving your goals.

Call in Ascended Master Merlin to help place his green energy over your goals in your mind or create a vision board and ask Ascended Master Merlin to place his magical and mystical green energy over your vision board to help achieve all your dreams and goals.

Keep asking and clearing away all negative emotional, feelings and train your thoughts to only think in a positive way to help become the sorcerer of your life.

79 Chemistry Within

*Start to look at ways in your life to
become a healthier you.*

Life is always about balance. It is for you to look at all aspects of how you are looking after yourself.

Are you eating nutritional food to fuel your body, eating regularly and mindfully eating? While eating, being grateful for the fresh food that you can access and eat.

Are you drinking fresh filtered water from a water container that's tin or glass? Trying to avoid drinking water from a plastic container. Drinking at least 2-3 litres of water daily to help your organs detox your body.

Do you have an addiction to caffeinated, sugary or alcoholic drinks? Can you consider starting to limit or cut back to help you limit the chemicals you are consuming?

Remembering our body health is our temple and what our souls is living in, without the health of our body our time here on Earth can be limited or comprised.

Is your gut health good? All our happy, positive hormones are created in our gut. A good probiotic is a great start to helping your chemistry within. Infrared saunas are a great way to help with detox your body from heavy minerals or any colds and flues you may have had recently. Exercise helps your body to stay strong, clears your thinking and a great way to help your lymph glands detox. Walking in nature or swimming in the ocean helps you mentally, spiritually, emotionally and physically.

Take some time to look at ways you can help your chemistry within to live your best life.

To live the life, you imaged and to have a long life, you need to keep your lifestyle clean. Start making little adjustments every day to help make a difference.

80 Enchanted

Look at life through magic and gratitude in your eyes.

See the world with eyes that's filled with magic and gratitude, it's amazing how your perception can change.

It's time for your life to become enchanted.

To do this, you must see and feel your life with magic and gratitude. Firstly, focus on letting go, of all the negative thoughts you may have about yourself and others. Through journaling or meditation start to purge all the negative emotions you have about yourself, family, friends and work colleges. Writing letters to purge your emotional baggage that you may have about a relationship in your past will help you release negative energy to help you become grateful. The letters are to be burnt as the letters are burning you are letting all the negative poisonous energy from your body and chakra system.

Become enchanted with your life, start to see the good in your life and the world. Vibing at a high vibration and a positive outlook helps your vibration, thus helping you attract opportunities and better situation and a higher quality of life.

Having gratitude and living in the present moment will make life magical. Being grateful for a flushing toilet, feeling blessed for the meal you are eating, taking time to watching a sunrise or sunset, with gratitude in your heart can create feelings of happiness.

If you can walk in a beautiful forest or soaking in the ocean can also help you become enchanted in the privilege of living your magical existence.

81 Soul's Journey

What's stirring in your soul, that you need to achieve, see, feel and do?

Start to look within your soul to feel what your lives mission is here on Earth. We can get caught up and life can pass you by with everyday chores of life.

Start to write down what you want to achieve in this lifetime, what you want to see, what you want to feel in your heart and soul and what you will feel proud of in your lifetime. Be mindful and make decisions so you don't leave this life with regret in your heart and soul. You can have a list or a vision board to capture what your soul wants to experience. Having a quiet moment with yourself every week is a great time to reflect on your soul's journey.

You are the captain of your ship, steering it toward your goals. Only you can decide what you want to achieve. If you are blaming a situation or someone else, look at letting that go. The difference between a person who has a fulfilling soul's journey is that they are in charge of planning their life. They corrects and adjusts their sails of their ship to achieve what they want to see, feel and experience in life.

Small steps everyday can make a difference. $27.50 wasted daily adds up to $10,000 per year. Buying a coffee daily is over $2000 per year. Would either of these amounts help you achieve one of your souls' desires. Rome was not built in a day, your life can look so different in 1 year, 3 year and 5 years.

It's time to start to take actions and live with no regrets.

Seize the day, my friend.

82 Your Holy Grail

*Ignite your spiritual purity. It's time to
ignite your purity within your soul.*

Your vessel – your earthly body to become a vessel that's filled with love, integrity and divine creator's light.

It's time to become an advocate for your own light, to become a warrior of what energy you allow in your body.

The holy grail has been linked to various knights of the round table. The divine creator is wanting you to bring the energy of the holy grail and the energy of the knights, the energy of high integrity for yourself, for you to start to have the belief that you can transform your life to feel the holy grail energy all around you to help enrich you and your family to have a blessed life with integrity, love and light all around you. It's time to feel and call in the energy of the holy grail into your body. Ask the knights of the holy grail to bring and ground into your body the golden energy to help raise your vibrations and by doing this, it's helping the energy of the planet to help elevate to 5th dimensional energy. The golden energy from the holy grail can also be sent to any problems you are having in your life; this golden light will help you find a solution or help you let go of the problem or help you see the situation in a different light. The holy grail is also associated with keeping the bloodlines of Jesus and Mary Magaline alive.

By anchoring the golden light of the holy grail into you and Earth, you are helping keep their energy alive and balancing the female and male energy here on Earth.

83 Trinity Healing

The trinity healing means to start to heal, awaken and to be conscious in all areas of your life.

In bibliology it means the father, son and the holy spirit. In a modern metaphysical way, it means to heal your physical self, your emotional self and your higher self.

It's now time to help heal the above areas of your life.

Start to be conscious of your own body. Do you eat nutritious food, filtered water, limiting chemicals and harmful processed foods into your body. This can lower your vibration and frequency. Are you exercising to help your body become stronger. Your soul self. Are you being authentic to your soul's journey. Are you living your life on your own terms or are you living up to everyone's expectations. Your soul is having an Earth experience, do you feel within yourself that you are achieving all the goals you wanted here on Earth. Take time to sit quietly to quieten the mind, meditate if you can, feel into your body, mind and spirit. Start to question yourself about where you are in life, feel into how your body is feeling when you are asking yourself these questions. What feelings and emotions are stirring in your soul. What's your gut instinct telling you.

Be brave, start to make changes to improve your life from what your souls telling you, listen to your body's guidance.

We create our world from our experiences, expectations and we think we deserve.

84 The Magi

Become wise – activate your wisdom.

The magi refers to the three wise men. Gold, frankincense and Myrrh. On a spiritual level is activating and asking the universal healers to bring all your spiritual gifts you have within your soul into your physical self and soul for this lifetime.

It's time to activate your magi of gifts.

Are you ready to remember, to allow and use the gifts you were given to flow back into you and your aura. To use them to help you within your life and to start to be of service to others.

Start to see your life in the divine creator's light and look at your life through the eyes of the creator. What can you change in your life to vibrate higher. Is it eating better, looking after yourself. Is it being aware of your self talk is it positive or negative or how do you allow other people to treat and talk to you. Meditate or sit at a beach or within a rainforest or somewhere close to you within nature and ask the universal healers to bring back or awaken within you, your Magi gifts. Take some deep breaths to allow these gifts to awaken within you and to allow them to start to active with your conscious mind. Start to journal what you are feeling. Do this for the next few weeks to see what spiritual gifts are activated. Take note of the changes you are making within your life.

Allow the magic of the magi to be awakened and to follow into your life. Once its help your life, see where you can help and be of service to others.

85 Master Lives

Calling in your past life's gifts.

Ask the universe for all your best qualities from your past lives to be given back you in this life now. You are now being prompted to start to transform your life into your best one yet, with a little help with some past life gifts reactivated into this life. We have had many hundreds of lives. In these past lives we have learnt many great qualities of leadership, strength, how to manifest, we've created wealth, and we've had lives with great loves and help others on many different scales.

It's time to bring back all of you master souls' qualities.

This exercise is to be done in a quiet space with no one around you.

> Take some deep breaths and ask your soul self to open and allow for the past life gifts that you are needing now at this stage of your life to come into your chakra system. Take some more breaths and allow this to happen now. An example for abundance would be, "Universal healers, I ask that my past lives gifts for abundance of wealth to be bought back to me in this lifetime."

> Take some breaths an allow this to happen. In your mind's eye, your third eye image seeing gold coins to flowing into your aura.

"So be it, that I allow and call back the gifts of wealth back into my life now." Thank the universal healers for their help.

You can ask and can do this process many times with the help of the universal healers to help you use all your soul gifts from many past lives.

Whatever you feel is lacking in your life, you can now ask and call back all your past life's gifts.

86 Goddess of Opportunity Lady Portia

Lady Portia is an ascended master who helps with justice and the goddess of opportunity.

Colour Vibration: golden light.

Helps the heart chakra, the thymus area.

Element – all elements -wind, earth, fire, and air.

Crystals to help Archangel clear quartz, rose quartz and Citrine.

Lady Portia is the ascended master who is on the board of karma, justice, and opportunity.

When you feel yourself or if you are helping a client and you feel you have or the client has been unfairly dealt a bad hand or something unjust has happened, ask Lady Portia to help you or the client. When she comes into my healing room, I see her in a beautiful golden gown, she's so beautiful, strong, and gracious. She taps the persons thymus area, their higher heart to clear any karma or to ignite their heart to find a solution or to attract the right help, the right person or to place them in the right place at the right time for good karma to happen to them.

When you see an opportunity for success in your life but have no idea how you will achieve this, ask Lady Portia. "Please help me achieve (say the goal or dream)." She loves people who try you achieve and create great opportunities for their lives.

If you or a person has been corrupted or know someone who has intentionally been mean to another person, Lady Portia can assist. You can ask her to help the authorities or whoever needs to know for the situation to be dealt with and for the innocent victim to be helped.

Lady Portia also loves placing her golden energy at your front door to help opportunities and achievements come to you and your family and for all the family to successfully achieve all their dreams and to follow their soul's purpose on Earth. You can also place her golden energy, if you own a business to help abundance and good karma to your business. If it is a business that has a front door, ask Lady Portia to place her golden energy at the front door and at the back door ask her to keep your success and abundance in your business. If it is an online business, ask Lady Portia to place her golden energy over your online business.

If you are struggling to forgive yourself or to forgive someone in your life, pray or meditate and ask Lady Portia to sit with you and ask her to clear your heart of hatred, hurt, sadness, humiliation, and any other low vibrational energy that you feel in your heart chakra. Ask her to place her golden energy in and around your heart chakra and your thymus area. Lady Portia also helps ease the heart chakra when families have lost a child and are experiences total heart break. Within your family DNA and past generations if you feel that there has been bad karma, you can pray, or meditate. Ask her to clear away family karma and bad energy between family members.

Lady Portia is such a blessing to call on to help you and your family. I know I am so grateful for all her help personally and in my healing room. If you are wanting to transform your life to become your best version of your earthly self, Lady Portia is the ascended master that can assist you.

BELOW IS A QR CODE TO A MEDITATION TO HELP YOU CONNECT WITH LADY PORTIA

87 Calling in your Higher Guidance

You are not alone here on your earthly journey.

We are all given a spirit guide, animal guides, higher vibrations parts of ourselves, elemental fairies and past over family members. We all have been assigned spiritual helpers for this life.

In a quiet place – walking, meditating or doing your favourite creative time, ask your team to help you connect with you and start to be given signs to know that they are with you. Just know every single day, your spiritual team are wanting to help you have your best life.

Ask your spiritual team to help you with all part of your life. To help you with your work, career, business and with your family, to help fill your heart with love and to see gratitude in all areas of your life. Spiritual dragons and unicorns have also come into the earthly realms since 2012 to help humans raise their vibrations from 3-dimensional energy to 5-7 dimensional levels. It's time now to ask to get to know your dragons and unicorns to help raise your vibrations and to start to ask to go ahead of you within your daily life to help you have a great day and to clear away any negative energy on your daily path, e.g. to help with a difficult work college or family member.

You have an assigned unicorn, that can help you to let go of any limiting physical problems like fatigue, tiredness or any other dis-ease your body is feeling. Ask your unicorn with their golden horn to touch and light up parts of your body the need help. This will activate a healing within your body.

To help have an even better connection to your spiritual team, let go of all old vibration energy. Emotional baggage can lower your vibrations. Ask the dragons to burn away all negative vibrations and stories that now longer serve you. Forgive and let go of low vibrational emotions, it's time to experience a better life. Letting go of old vibrations will help you raise your vibration for your spiritual team to be easier to connect and for you to hear and feel their guidance.

Take time in your life to meditate or journal to help become centred and focused on clearing away old feelings, emotions and any forms of unhappiness with your life.

Just remember you are not alone, and you have a spiritual team to help, love and assist you in all aspects of your life. Take time to get to feel them and listen to their guidance.

88 Untangled Energy

It's time to clear your energy daily from others.

Are you feeling drained from others? Here are some techniques to help you. This is great to do daily, to help you clear peoples overlaid energy, negative thoughts and feelings from others and sadness you may feel from others.

This technique is best to do in a private place.

1. Ask the divine creator for a column of white light all around you.
2. Imagine and feel the white column of light expanding to a metre around you.
3. Once you feel or imagine the white light, ask Archangel Michael to step into the column of white light.
4. Ask Archangel Michael to clear away any energy from other people.
5. You can feel or imagine Archangel Michael cutting cords or removing layers of energy from you, like an onion.

If you keep thinking about a person or situation, ask Archangel Michael to help remove the cords and energy from you. Archangel Michael can also help you if you feel cranky or having negative thoughts or keep going over a negative conversation you have had with someone, just do the same process with the white light and asking Archangel Michael to help you.

Once you have cleared negative energy, thank Archangel Micheal for his time and then ask Archangel Michael for his blue cloak of protection. The blue cloak of protection is great to ask daily for to help you stop feeling drained from family, friends, work colleges or from being amongst other people.

It's time for you to stand in your power, to feel confident and strong. To do good things here on Earth you have to be clear, focused and in the divine creator's light.

It's time to shine in the light and in your own soul's power.

89 Merlin Dragon

Helping ground the merlin energy into Earth.

You are being introduced to the Merlin dragon and its magnificent energy. This is to help you feel like you have been 'freed' from your limiting thoughts and feelings about yourself and your life circumstances. The stories from this era are that the merlin dragon was chained beneath Camelot by Uther. The dragon has been sent by Ascended Master Merlin from the heavens to help you free you from your limiting thoughts, feelings, fears of lack in your life.

> It's time to step into your true soul self of love, abundance and unlimited self-belief that this lifetime anything is possible for you to achieve and create.

The Merlin dragon is now with you to help bring magic and mystery into your daily life.

Ask your Merlin dragon to help protect your energy from other people's negative emotions or negative overlaid energy. Nightly, you can ask the Merlin dragon to help clear away and cut cords from everyone you have been in contact with or thought off. Your Merlin dragon can also send energy ahead of you for the day, this can help you have an easier day with less stress and to help your day flow with ease and grace. You can also ask your Merlin dragon to help find your dream home or a better job. A great suggestion is to ask your Merlin dragon to place you in the right place at the right time to help find what you are needing in life.

The Merlin dragons have come to Earth to help raise the vibration of the Earth by helping reignite the energy of magic and mystery back into people's belief system.

90 Earth Star Abundance

Abundance is all around you.

Do you feel like you are destined for great things in this lifetime. If you do not feel like this, it's time to change the way you are thinking and feeling. The divine creator is wanting you to step into your abundance and wisdom that is stored in your Earth Star.

Your Earth Star is located one metre below your feet, in Mother Earth. In your Earth Star has all your past lives abundance, wisdom, knowledge and good fortune is store here.

You have been given this information to ask for what you are needing in this lifetime. Ask your Earth Star to awaken and to activate for what you are needing now. What are you needing help with to bring abundance and wisdom with right now.

Ask the divine creator for a column of white light all the way down to your Earth Star. Now ask your Earth Star to release into your body and aura all the abundance, wisdom and gifts you are needing.

You can visualise beautiful golden and red energy being absorbed from your Earth Star into your chakra system. Start to feel your chakra system awaken and activate all that you are needing to achieve your dreams and goals.

Take some deep breaths and breath into your body and chakra system strength from your Earth Star and allowing it to be stored into your body now. This is also a great exercise to do if you feel like you are unsettled or feel like you can't concentre on the tasks.

Try to ground your energy into your Earth Star. Take notice and see your life change by grounding your energy into your Earth Star daily.

BELOW IS A QR CODE TO A MEDITATION
TO HELP YOU CLEAR AND INCREASE YOUR
VIBRATION IN YOUR EARTH STAR CHAKRA

91 Unicorn Healing

Today you are reconnecting with your unicorn.

Since 2012 everyone on Earth has been given a unicorn to help awaken and heal everyone's heart chakra. This is to help raise the vibration within you and around the planet. All unicorns are linked to Archangel Mary, the mother of all. The unicorns and Archangel Mary help heal the heart chakra hurts and to strengthen your self-worth.

Your unicorn with their golden horn wants to touch all your chakras today to heal and light up your chakra system. Take time now to allow your unicorn to awaken your chakra system.

Everyday get to know your unicorn. Your unicorn will tell you their name, they are here to help you become the best version of yourself by helping your heart charka heal and become your strongest chakra. Sit with your new friendly unicorn and let them release all the heart chakra hurts or hurts from all your chakras. Take some deep breaths and release to your unicorns, all the times someone has hurt your feelings, said hurtful words, made a negative comment. With your breaths release these to your unicorns now.

Take the time for your unicorn to help raise your vibration. Release old hurts, helps raise your vibration to help your soul love yourself more to help attract a higher vibrational life partner or to help you find a better life path.

Know that you now have a loving unicorn by your side to help you raise your heart vibration and always love and support you.

SCAN THE QR CODE TO CONNECT WITH YOUR ELEMENTALS, UNICORNS, AND DRAGONS

92 Sun Strength

*It's time to balance your divine masculine
and your feminine energies.*

The great central sun is the divine masculine Helios and the divine feminine Vesta. They are both coming forth today to be with you to activate your strengths from the central sun. They are here to bless your body with strength, to activate your souls' downloads and learnings. Allow the great central sun energy to activate and ignite oneness and strength within.

Take a few minutes to allow this to flow in now. If you feel you have become too sensitive to your environment – physically, emotionally and mentally, this will help you to reset, recap and renew your energy, to enjoy Earth again.

Allow yourself to sit in the divine creator's white light, now ask the energy from the great central sun to pour over you, golden white light. This light is healing your vibrational force field to help you rise above all the negative emotions and energies that is making your body and emotions sensitive.

Feel all the lower vibrations drop away from you now. The light is now raising you higher and higher. Your vibrations will keep rising to help you heal and become stronger and stronger.

This healing energy from the central sun is also balancing your masculine and feminine energy. Giving you back balance to your emotional and physical body to help you become your best version.

Call on the great central sun and their golden light energy to give physical and emotional strength anytime you are needing it.

93 Full Moon Energy

It's time to learn to embrace the rituals of the moon and to embrace your feminine aspects.

A great ritual to embrace, is on the full moon purge, let go of any emotions that no longer serve you. In a letter form, write down all your emotions, feelings and thoughts that are keeping you thinking negative thoughts or making you sad. These thoughts are keeping your vibrational energy low. Once you have written the letter you burn the letter on the full moon, as you are burning the letter, you feel and allow all your emotions to be release from your body. Give it to the moon energies to release or healed and bought back to you in a higher vibrational form.

Around the full moon is a great time to declutter your home, get rid of things that you have no longer need or hold old emotions that no longer serves you.

The full moon is a great time to smudge your home or burn incense, light candles or burn essential oils to clear away negative energy from your home or workspace.

If you have crystals place them in the full moon light to help clear away negative energy they have absorbed or to help raise their vibrational energy.

It's a great time to have a fire inside your fire place or a fire outside in the full moon and sit in the full moon to help reactivate your feminine strength. With your mind's eye release into the fire, all the emotions that no longer serves you.

Sit in the moon light, bath in her glorious energy, walking or watching the sun set and the full moon rise is so healing and groundling for your soul.

94 New Moon Healing

*A new moon can help for the new
you to emerge within you.*

Transformation can take time, every new moon write and set some goals and intentions to achieve in the moon cycle.

You can write your list of intentions and place it in a tray in the new moon, if its money you are wanting to manifest, place a gold coin on the tray. If its love, place a heart and the list of what you are wanting to have in your next partner. If it's a physical goal place the number, you want to see on the scales for the next full moon cycle.

This is a great time to re-organise your home to make way for a more organise systems and ways you feel about yourself and within your home.

If your emotions are out of balance, this is a reminder to ask the feminine moon to help you have a nourishing sleep to give you strength physically and emotionally or help fulfil your goals and intentions.

Visualise on a new moon, how your perfect day will flow and all the healthy activities you want to have, how you feel every day and you interreact with friends, family and colleges.

If it's abundance you want in your life or business, blowing cinnamon out the front door of your home or place of business on the night of a new moon and writing what abundance you want to bring into your home or place of business, placing the list under the door mat at the front door is a great way to help bring in abundance.

Our life is one big cycle, change is our only constant in life, look at our beautiful moon, how she is constantly changing.

95 Sovereignty Within

It's time to align with your sovereignty within you, for your highest good to shine.

A meaning for sovereignty is freedom from external control, free from control of others.

> It is time for you to take power and control of your life. To clear the slate of any negative thoughts, experiences, emotions and regrets.

To step into your true sovereignty to let go of all the things that are holding you back.

Be brave and start to make a list of all that takes away your power, happiness and joy.

Do you need to write some purge letters to let go off hurts from your past relationships and family members. The emotions you feel are poisoning your body with the negative emotions you are feeling and thinking. Do you need to contact someone to apologies and say sorry? Are you employed by a company that doesn't align with your beliefs, values and morals? Does your body make you feel uncomfortable, or does it limit you doing the things you are wanting to do or achieve. It is time to get your physical power back? Do you give your power away to others, by worrying what other people think about you?

Start to make changes and to run your own race, to stay in your own lane and empowering yourself.

It's time to step into your sovereignty – financially, physically, emotionally and spiritually.

96 Becoming Self Sufficient and Respecting Mother Earth

Awaken your conscience, to helping honour and be the most thoughtful human you can be to protect Mother Earth.

We all need to help Mother Earth where we can and become more self-sufficient.

The Mother of Earth is screaming for our help.

In your life, where can you make a difference.

Can you grow a vegetable garden, plant fruit trees, have a few chooks, get solar panels or your own water tanks? Everyday look to how you can help make a difference and less of an impact on Earth. Are you using bleaches and harmful chemicals in your home? Can you change to natural cleaners or even vinegar and essential oils to clean with. Can you be more conscious of what products to buy and limit the amount of waste in packaging you are throwing away. Being also conscious of trying not to over purchase food for your home and stop throwing away out of day food will make a difference. Can you walk or carpool to work? To help with car emissions. Take note and start to think how you and the company you work for can help lessen their overuses and helping lessen the environmental impact we are having on Mother Earth. Can you save water in your home or look at getting water tanks to help with water usage. Be mindful when purchasing clothes. So much of our earth's resources are wasted on clothing production and then larges amount of land waste contains used clothing, when takes years to biodegrade. Installing a water filtration system and filling up a glass or tin reuseable water bottle instead of buying plastic water bottles will make an impact or a keep cup for your hot drinks.

Maybe one person will not make a difference but if you start and then you encourage a friend to become conscious to Mother Earth and then you ask them to pass it onto to another friend, you are creating a ripple effect, and this will help our Mother Earth.

About the Author

Joanne Plater is an Intuitive Healer that has used her clairvoyant and psychic abilities to help thousands of clients awaken to their higher self and potential. She is a Spiritual Course facilitator as well as a qualified Natural Therapies Practitioner, Meditation facilitator, Holistic Councillor, Reiki Master / facilitator and Clairvoyant.

Joanne owns a wellness centre called Alchemy in Bellingen on the mid north coast of New South Wales, Australia. Here, she sees clients weekly and facilitates courses in Clairvoyant Development, Spiritual Development, Inner Child Workshops and Manifesting.

Her connection with the heavens has always been clear, even when she was a child. Joanne's soul was born into her body in 1975, and while her parents accepted her weird questions, they didn't want her to look or act differently to other children. She was blessed to grow up on a farm that overlooked the stunning Blue Mountains, and their property lay next to the Nepean River. She grew up with lots of farm animals and loved being outside with them.

Every year that passed, Joanne realised she was a little different to most. She had many imaginary friends, that she now knows were her spirit guides and angelic team. She started attending a spiritual development course at 27 that helped her have a better connection to her higher self, her spiritual team and to learn how to meditate.

Joanne's passion is helping people awaken and evolve to their highest potential and to help her clients be aware of their soul lessons here on Earth. She has a gift that enables her to move back and forth on a clients' timeline, clearly seeing what needs healing and clearing from their past and also allows them to see what life lessons lay ahead. She then heals through the Chakra System and with the assistants of the Ascended masters.

Joanne has been blessed by an amazing connection with her spiritual team. When she's preparing for a day of clients, she will meditate in the morning and her spiritual team will advise her as to what she needs to address with each client. This is an amazing gift as she can see up to 20 clients per week, it is like a literal download of each person's story.

So many people are living in their past and not living their best life. Joanne inspires and motivates them to help improve the way they think and to clear negative energy from their chakra system.

Her next step in helping Earth raise its vibration is becoming an author.

www.ingramcontent.com/pod-product-compliance
Lightning Source LLC
Chambersburg PA
CBHW060354080526
44583CB00012B/314